"I have great news for the reader—Tommy Newberry has written an incredible book! And he is absolutely right: What you think about yourself determines who you are; therefore, think strategically. *Success Is Not an Accident* helps us understand why success can be achieved by any person, in any situation, under any circumstance, but never by accident! You should read this book if you are setting big goals for enhancing your life and intentionally charting the path to make those big goals a reality. Let's impact our world!"

Dan T. Cathy, president and COO, Chick-fil-A, Inc.

"Tommy Newberry provides a powerful approach for attaining personal success in all of life's arenas. The philosophy and methods outlined in *Success Is Not an Accident* focus on the direct ways individuals can achieve their God-given potential. Tommy represents the very best in the crowded field of life coaching, and I have benefited tremendously from his work."

J. Rex Fuqua, president and CEO, Fuqua Capital Corporation

"This enjoyable, fast-moving book is full of great ideas and insights anyone can use to enjoy a better life."

Brian Tracy, author of *The Way to Wealth*

"If you are tired of responding to life and ready to start creating it, then I encourage you to read this book. Success doesn't happen by accident. It happens by making the decision to be the driver of your bus and charting your course to a destination called Success. Thankfully, Tommy Newberry provides us with a map that will take us where we want to go."

Jon Gordon, author of *The Energy Bus: 10 Rules to Fuel Your Life, Work, and Team with Positive Energy*

"*Success Is Not an Accident* overflows with life-changing, practical wisdom. I really like the stories, the succinct lists of action steps, and the powerful principles that translate purpose into practical reality. Read this book and you'll have crystal-clear strategies and tools for unlocking your God-given potential."

Dr. Tim Irwin, corporate psychologist and author of *Run with the Bulls without Getting Trampled*

"Authentic success happens only through focus and intentionality. I learned this truth from Tommy Newberry. We all have a responsibility to push beyond our comfort zones and maximize our positive influence at home, at work, and in the community. This book is easy to read and clearly shows you how to get from where you are today to where God wants you to be. I've benefited directly from working with Tommy, and you will too when you read and apply the lessons in *Success Is Not an Accident.*"

Dr. Vic Pentz, senior pastor, Peachtree Presbyterian Church, Atlanta, Georgia

Success Is Not an Accident

SUCCESS
IS NOT AN
ACCIDENT

TOMMY NEWBERRY

 Tyndale House Publishers, Inc., Carol Stream, Illinois

Visit Tyndale's exciting Web site at www.tyndale.com

TYNDALE and Tyndale's quill logo are registered trademarks of Tyndale House Publishers, Inc.

The 1% Club, Success Is Not an Accident, and America's Success Coach are registered trademarks of The 1% Club, Inc. All rights reserved.

Success Is Not an Accident: Change Your Choices, Change Your Life

Copyright © 1999, 2007 by Tommy Newberry. All rights reserved.

Cover photo copyright © by Matthias Kulka/Corbis. All rights reserved.

Author photo copyright © 2006 by Ted Domohowski. All rights reserved.

Designed by Jennifer Ghionzoli

Scripture quotations marked NLT are taken from the *Holy Bible,* New Living Translation, copyright © 1996, 2004. Used by permission of Tyndale House Publishers, Inc., Carol Stream, Illinois 60188. All rights reserved.

Scripture quotations marked NIV are taken from the HOLY BIBLE, NEW INTERNATIONAL VERSION®. NIV®. Copyright © 1973, 1978, 1984 by International Bible Society. Used by permission of Zondervan. All rights reserved.

Scripture quotations marked NKJV are taken from the New King James Version®. Copyright © 1982 by Thomas Nelson, Inc. Used by permission. All rights reserved. *NKJV* is a trademark of Thomas Nelson, Inc.

Published in association with the literary agency of The Knight Agency, 557 S. Main St., Madison, GA 30650

Library of Congress Cataloging-in-Publication

Newberry, Tommy.
  Success is not an accident / Tommy Newberry.
    p. cm.
  Includes bibliographical references and index.
  ISBN-13: 978-1-4143-1311-5 (sc : alk. paper)
  ISBN-10: 1-4143-1311-X (sc : alk. paper)
    1. Success. 2. Success—Religious aspects—Christianity. I. Title.
BF637.S8N435 2007
158.1—dc22   2006103497

Printed in the United States of America

13 12 11 10 09 08 07

7 6 5 4 3 2 1

This book is lovingly dedicated to

*Mom and Dad and
my sisters, Cindy, Suzanne, Jenny, and Beth*

By Tommy Newberry

BOOKS

The 4:8 Principle

Success Is Not an Accident

366 Days of Wisdom & Inspiration

AUDIO

Success Is Not an Accident: Secrets of the Top 1%

Order your copy at www.tommynewberry.com

CP0114

CONTENTS

ACKNOWLEDGMENTS

Writing a book is a monumental project. Although the author's name appears on the cover, it requires a team of dedicated people behind the scenes to make the undertaking a success. As I've learned over the years, few significant accomplishments can ever be completed alone, and this book is no exception. Though it would be virtually impossible to list all the people who have influenced me and contributed to *Success Is Not an Accident,* I want to recognize a special few who helped make this book possible.

First, I must thank the members of The 1% Club for their many suggestions, observations, and insights over the past fifteen years. I may hold the title of coach, but in reality I am still very much a student.

Thank you to Dick Parker, who helped me develop the original version of this book. Special thanks to my agent, Pamela Harty, who believed in me and in this project and helped make it all happen. Thanks to Carol Traver and Dave Lindstedt, from Tyndale, who caught the vision for this project and patiently provided productive feedback and sound advice. Thank you to my business partner, Steve Cesari, whose perspective and life experience added a new dimension to this updated version of *Success Is Not an Accident.*

Thanks to my parents, whose unconditional love, encouragement, and affirmation freed me to chart my own course and follow my dream. As the years go by, my appreciation grows for the example they set and the wisdom they passed down.

Boundless thanks to my wife, Kristin, who never let me forget how much she believed in me as I worked through the original manuscript, and more recently, as I completed the updates for this book and at the same time finished my next book, *The 4:8 Principle.*

Foremost, I want to thank God for my special combination of talents, gifts, and life experiences, as well as for the inspiration and creativity that allowed this book to become a reality.

INTRODUCTION

If you want to take your business, your marriage, or your entire life from good to great, *Success Is Not an Accident* will help you get there, perhaps faster than you ever dreamed possible. This book provides the launching pad you've been looking for. Whether you are seeking to grow your net worth or rebuild your self-worth, these principles and strategies will help you do just that. How can I be so sure?

The seven lessons in this book represent the foundation curriculum that I have been using in my coaching practice at The 1% Club since 1991. Together, the seven lessons represent a complete system for managing your life more effectively. In this updated and expanded version of *Success Is Not an Accident,* I have distilled and incorporated the most valuable insights from my clients, as well as the lessons I have learned in the process of coaching them. If you like, think of these lessons as the secrets of the top 1% of successful people. They're not really secrets, though. They just appear to be secrets because so few people pay attention to these principles or seriously set out to practice them. While the principles are quite simple, the results you can expect to achieve are quite remarkable!

The book you hold in your hands contains the absolute best ideas for getting from where you are now to where you really want to be in life. Just as professional and Olympic athletes have coaches, I want to be your success coach, your trainer for life. My passion is to help you become a world-class human being, someone who pulls out all the stops in each area of life.

Success Is Not an Accident is not a book about living the way most people live. You don't need a book to do that; it happens by default. If you live your life like most people do, you will get what most people get and settle for what they settle for. Here's a taste of most people's experience:

- Currently, 49 percent of marriages end in divorce.

- More than 80 percent of people working today would rather be in another line of work.

- More than 50 percent of Americans are overweight.

- One out of three Americans will get cancer, and two out of five will suffer from heart disease.

- More than 60 percent of Americans, who live in the richest, most abundant civilization in history, will retire with little or no savings and will become dependent on so-called entitlements for survival.

No one plans to become mediocre. Rather, mediocrity is the result of no plan at all. Let me give you a simple but true formula: *If you want to lead an extraordinary life, find out what the ordinary do—and don't do it.*

When I first wrote and self-published *Success Is Not an Accident* in 1999, I was certain that the principles I was teaching would be helpful and exceedingly practical to any reader committed to putting them into regular practice. At the time of my initial writing, I had been coaching successful entrepreneurs and their families for more than six years. When I wasn't coaching, I found myself obsessed with researching the life stories of men and women who had put these timeless principles into action in their own lives. I consumed everything I could read or listen to that might help me better understand what makes some people unusually happy and successful. On the personal side, I had been married for three years and had been a dad for just two.

Since its initial release, *Success Is Not an Accident* has sold more than one hundred thousand copies, primarily through old-fashioned word of mouth, and it has now been translated into three languages. For the most part, this has happened quietly, gradually, and virtually unnoticed in the world of books and self-improvement. This "best-kept secret," as many of my clients refer to it, has slipped under the radar and positively influenced thousands of lives with its simple, direct, and no-nonsense approach to maximizing one's full potential. Now, ten years later, I am in my sixteenth year of what is commonly referred to as life coaching, and I'm loving every minute of it. I just celebrated my thirteenth year of marriage to my wife, Kristin, and together we are raising three boys—eleven and nine years old, and eighteen months. The challenges of life are more fun than ever. I feel very blessed indeed.

I have invested my entire adult life in studying and teaching the causes of peak performance. Since first writing this book, however, I have learned far more than I have taught. In working with entrepreneurs, CEOs, and business leaders in more than thirty different industries, as well as coaching hundreds of happy couples from numerous backgrounds, I have learned what it takes to turn around a business, a marriage, and a life. I have learned what it takes to get rid of the mental, emotional, and physical clutter that bogs down most people and robs them of the life satisfaction they crave. I have learned what it takes to experience the fulfillment that comes from living in sync with one's God-given purpose. I have learned what it takes to double, triple, or even quadruple your income in as little as two or three years. Better yet, I have learned what it takes to work less and still earn more. Most importantly, though, I've learned that success is most definitely *not* an accident! With another ten years of field experience under my belt, I am more convinced than ever that success is absolutely predictable. Success happens for a reason!

When you incorporate the principles from each lesson of *Success Is Not an Accident* into your daily life, you will begin to experience the same explosive results my clients have repeatedly experienced. I have seen this happen over and over again, yet from time to time it still amazes me. I've seen the concepts you're about to learn work for busy sales executives as well as stay-at-home moms. I've seen the principles work in golf, baseball, martial arts, and other athletic endeavors. I've seen them work for ambitious high-school students, those fresh out of college, and those earning six- or seven-figure incomes. I've seen the system work for both male and female clients. I have seen it work for my single clients as well as my clients who are married with kids. I can assure you that this life-management system will work for you to the exact degree that you apply its principles consistently in your day-to-day life.

This book, in essence, contains a formula that has been proven to generate positive, predictable results. I encourage you to blend my formula with your personality to create your own unique personal-success system. I want you to put your own slant on the concepts in this book, as long as you strictly abide by the principles. In other words, focus on the spirit of the law rather than just the letter. Whether your aspiration is to start your own business, earn straight A's in school, move into your dream home, get lean, run a marathon, become a schoolteacher, generate millions in sales, put your faith into practice, or set a better example for your kids—the principles are still the same. And these principles of effective living are nonnegotiable. Universal principles work in our lives whether we like them, understand them, or even know about them. You can be confident that the principles taught in each lesson are built upon the firm foundation of truth. They are not untested theories or my particular opinions; instead, they are based on personal experience and extensive observation. The concepts that underlie this system are proven steps to both enjoying and succeeding in the game of life.

I've observed that when individuals stray from timeless principles, adversity of some kind is never far behind. You can discern this for yourself with children and adults alike. Unwavering principles govern each area of our lives. When we attempt to bend, stretch, or otherwise pervert them, we set ourselves up for inescapable pain and regret sooner or later. The most successful individuals who ever lived have resisted the natural human tendency to make up their own laws of life. Likewise, if you want to develop all your potential, you must avoid the trendy "principle of the day" mentality that has permeated our society. The Bible gives a clear promise for those who remember God's universal principles: "Joyful are people of integrity, who follow the instructions of the LORD" (Psalm 119:1, NLT).

The good news about universal principles is that they will always be there for you. No matter how often you abandon or slander them, they will still welcome you back, like the father of the Prodigal Son, with open arms. Naturally, you will still experience the repercussions of getting off track, but the right course will be only a principle or two away.

The principles supporting each lesson in this book can be compared to the fundamentals in baseball—moving the runner along, hitting the cutoff man, throwing strikes. The baseball team that adheres to the fundamentals most consistently wins most consistently. It is really no mystery. Even a talent-packed team of superstars will stop winning when they fail to execute the proper fundamentals. By refocusing on the basics, individuals as well as teams can break out of slumps.

View the lessons in this book as your playbook for successful living. They describe the essentials for living a remarkable life. Putting them into practice consistently is the prerequisite for designing a life worth living. This playbook also includes a variety of drills and exercises that will sharpen your understanding and application.

For the rest of *Success Is Not an Accident*, allow me to be your personal life coach. As I tell my clients, my job is to help you get the most out of yourself. My goal is to help you reach your goals. Throughout each lesson in this book, I will challenge you to be the best you can be. I've tried to write with an underlying tone of encouragement and accountability.

Sometimes, like any good coach, I may appear blunt or even harsh. Don't take it personally. I just don't want to let you off the hook. I do not want to see you cheat yourself and your family out of the fruits of your full potential.

Throughout this book, I will give you new information, new perspectives, new strategies, and new skills. I will break down the complex into the simple. Each lesson includes practical and usable methods for improving your performance. Sometimes, though, I won't be teaching you anything new; I'll just be reminding you of what you need to do and exactly when you need to do it.

I hope you will implement the entire system laid out in this book. If you do, it will change your life forever. Each lesson is a component of the entire system. While you will make significant gains by applying only one or two lessons, you will amaze yourself and others if you put the complete system into action. When you fully integrate the system into every area of your life, you will experience a surge of confidence, competence, and unparalleled optimism for the future. The responsibility for implementing it, though, is all yours. I cannot do it for you, and you cannot hire anyone else to do it for you. It is completely up to you.

Finally, in writing this book, I hope to further my personal mission of positively impacting people's lives by teaching the timeless, proven principles of successful living. I do not claim to be superior in any way. In fact, you probably have many natural talents and past accomplishments that are greater than my own. I simply have a burning desire to share the truth about success with others. These truths existed long before I came into this world, and they will survive long after I am gone. Even though others may call you lucky, if you put into practice the principles that follow, you need not be surprised when you succeed. Success is in your hands. The seeds of greatness lie within us all. It is only when we stop believing that a better life is possible that we begin to settle for less.

Please share your success stories with me by sending them to www.successisnotanaccident.com. I look forward to hearing from you!

ABOUT THE FORMAT

The format of this book is designed specifically to help you understand and retain the material. For example, many of the right-hand pages contain diagrams, call-out text, and drawings that reinforce the principles you are learning. Also, the opening page to each lesson includes a rundown of the benefits you will receive by incorporating the principles that follow, and a closing page suggests assignments that will help you integrate the lessons into your daily life.

This book was intended not just to be read but to be internalized. It will give you not only knowledge but also immediately usable strategies for living a balanced, significant life. As you read, make notes in the margin, underline key points, and highlight what you want to remember. Reread the pages that seem to be speaking directly to you. I also encourage you to teach what you most want to learn—nothing will accelerate your progress faster! Whether it is a peer, spouse, child, close friend, or business partner, find a receptive person whom you can regularly influence with the ideas from *Success Is Not an Accident*. I'll prompt you to do this at the end of each lesson.

With the encouragement of Tyndale House Publishers, I am thrilled to be introducing this updated and expanded version of *Success Is Not an Accident*. This book is written for you and for those like you, who look to God and themselves as the solution to their problems and the path to an exceptional, meaningful life here on earth.

The strategies and insights on the pages that follow can be the difference between an ordinary life and an extraordinary life.

Now let's get started.

Choose Success

Your success blesses others!

In this lesson, you will learn to

- Clarify your concept of success

- Accept complete responsibility

- Eliminate excuses forever

- Become a doer, not a feeler

- Develop an abundance mentality

Success is not an accident! This is, without a doubt, the single most important lesson you must grasp if you want to maximize your full potential and enjoy all the fulfillment and success you were designed to enjoy. Success occurs in the lives of specific people for specific reasons. It is not something that randomly happens to you; it is something that you make happen. This is exciting news! Whether you want to strengthen your family life, improve your career, deepen your faith, or take your physical energy to a whole new level, you can do it. Ralph Waldo Emerson writes, "Let him learn a prudence of a higher strain. Let him learn that every thing in nature, even motes and feathers, go by law and not by luck, and that what he sows he reaps."[1]

There is no magic. This process is not complex or sophisticated. If you will invest the time to find out what other people have done to be successful, personally and professionally, and then begin doing the same things, you too will achieve similar results in due season. All your efforts will be worthwhile!

Hit the Bull's-Eye!

Imagine trying to throw darts at a dartboard in a room with no lights on. Even in the dark, you would eventually hit the board, and if you continued for long enough, you would probably hit the bull's-eye. But if you turned on the lights, gathered a large supply of darts, got some coaching, and invested ample time in practicing, you would significantly reduce the time it would take to hit the dartboard. When you finally hit the bull's-eye, many people would call you lucky. But you wouldn't be lucky. You would just have been willing to do more things to ensure that you hit the bull's-eye.

This book was designed to help you identify the factors within your control that will increase the odds of your hitting the bull's-eye in your own journey through life.

What's Your Dream?

When you were growing up, did you ever dream of being a professional athlete? I wanted to be a baseball player. I can easily recall playing out

World Series scenarios in the backyard with my friends until it was too dark to see the ball. But what separates the kids who dream about playing in the World Series from those who actually grow up to win the pennant? Sure, it has to do with talent, ability, and a bit of good timing, but I also believe it has a great deal to do with sheer determination and work ethic.

If you had seen him playing Little League, you never would have guessed that Orel Hershiser would someday become one of the greatest pitchers in baseball history. But it was at the age of eight, while visiting Yankee Stadium in New York, that Hershiser set his goal. "It was while walking into that historic stadium on a crisp, windy night that I decided I wanted to be a big league baseball player," he said.[2] It's a dream many little boys have had, but it was a goal that Hershiser would prove to be serious about achieving.

STRIKE ONE, STRIKE TWO

As a freshman in high school, Hershiser started to develop a plan for reaching his goal. First, he wanted to make the varsity baseball team. But he fell short of his goal twice, and it was not until his junior year that he earned a spot on the varsity team.

When applying to colleges, Hershiser set his sights on playing for Bowling Green State University. But once again, things didn't turn out the way he planned. When it came time to try out for the team, Hershiser was academically ineligible. With his college aspirations hitting rock bottom, he left school. On the bus ride home, Hershiser made a critical decision: "The boy on the bus to Michigan was not the man I wanted to be."[3] He would not be a quitter.

Hershiser returned to Bowling Green for the summer session and played for an amateur baseball team. In his junior year, he finally made the school's traveling team and became a starting pitcher. Now he hoped the scouts in the stands would notice him.

THE CALL

Hershiser was noticed. In 1979, the Los Angeles Dodgers picked him in the seventeenth round of the amateur draft. But as a Class A player, his chances of making it to the majors were slim. Only 4 percent of those drafted ever make it out of the minor leagues. It took four and a half years of playing in the minors before Hershiser received the call he'd been working toward since he was eight. In 1983, he was called up to the big leagues.

NEW GOALS

As a major-league player, Hershiser continued to work hard at improving his game, and after five years in the majors, he set a new goal for himself: He wanted to be the youngest, smartest major-league pitcher ever.[4]

His new goal was realized in 1988. After recovering from knee surgery and an emergency appendectomy, Hershiser went on to have the season of a lifetime. He broke Don Drysdale's "unbreakable" record by pitching fifty-nine consecutive scoreless innings. He was named Most Valuable Player of the National League Championship Series and the World Series, and he received a Gold Glove and the Cy Young Award.

AFTER THE GAME

During the excitement of the 1988 season, Robert Fraley, Hershiser's friend and sports representative, told him, "You're about to make a lot of money. But that is not true success. Success will be measured at the end of your career, not at the peak. When you're finished with baseball, if you love God, if you're still in love with your wife, if your children know who you are, and if your reputation is still intact, then you'll be successful."[5] Hershiser adopted his friend's definition of success and emphasized it in interviews: "When I'm finished with my baseball career, my most successful goal is not to make the Hall of Fame, but to see my family a success as a result of my influence in their lives."[6]

In June 2000, Hershiser retired from baseball with a record of 204 wins as a pitcher, nineteen years as a faithful husband, and fifteen years as an involved dad. He once said, "I'm proof that great things can happen to ordinary people if they work hard and never give up."[7] And that is the reality of success.

Was Orel Hershiser just lucky? I don't think so! Consider these other heroes who succeeded:

Was Tiger Woods just lucky?

Was Bill Gates just lucky?

Was Roger Clemens just lucky?

Was Carrie Underwood just lucky?

Was J. K. Rowling just lucky?

Was Rick Warren just lucky?

Was Lance Armstrong just lucky?

Were the immigrants who came to America with nothing but determination in their pockets but who built a fortune by serving others just lucky?

Are the Super Bowl champions each year just lucky?

Are Olympic medalists just lucky?

Success is not an accident, and it's not based on luck. That statement is simple, and it's the truth. And the moment you fully accept it, your life and the lives of those you love will never again be the same. Success, however it's defined, is absolutely predictable.

Get Clear on Success

What does success mean to *you*? Answering this question is one of the first assignments I give my coaching clients in The 1% Club. Investing the time and effort to define success in your own terms is one of the most helpful mental and spiritual exercises you can undertake. If you are trying to accelerate your success, it only makes sense to first define the target, which in many cases is elusive and often misunderstood.

What exactly does success mean to you? I've observed that most people find it quite difficult to define. But if you don't have a clear picture of success, how can you honestly pursue it or expect to achieve and then enjoy it? Success has been defined many ways in literature:

- Success is the progressive realization of a worthy ideal.

- Success is the accomplishment of God's will in your life.

- Success is making the most of what you have.

- Success is who you become.

- Success is living your life in your own way.

- Success is a journey.

These definitions vary, but I suppose there is a dose of truth in each one. The most successful people in the world are those who have taken the time to figure out exactly who they want to become and what they want to achieve. Then they invest the hours of their days in activities consistent with these ideals.

Successful people are those who have learned how to consistently apply God's laws in their lives. They ascribe their achievements to focus, hard work, strong relationships, perseverance, and the blessing of God. The unsuccessful or mediocre are those who have no obvious direction. These people tend to "go with the flow" or drift in whichever direction the wind happens to be blowing. Their lives are dominated by circumstances and overflowing with excuses. They blame their underachievement on bad luck. Life, they claim, has dealt them a bad hand, and they choose to fold.

ARE YOU SUCCESSFUL?

How do you define success? That is the real question! Do you equate it with wealth? Do you believe you are successful if you have a lot of friends, or is it social status that matters? Do you think you are a success if you own a nice home, a car, or other worthwhile possessions? If you're active in your church and tithe regularly, does that signify success? Does power bring success, or will accomplishing the next goal on your list finally usher in success? Maybe success is early retirement, or maybe it comes when all the kids have gone away to college or have married and started their own families. What exactly is success to you? Before I push you any further, let me ask you a different but vitally important question.

DOES GOD EVEN WANT YOU TO SUCCEED?

Many people of faith wonder whether it's wrong to pursue wealth or certain types of worldly success. Some even feel guilty for wanting what others don't have. What about you? Do you think God wants you to succeed? Really dig deep and answer this question.

Here is my answer in the form of another question: Do you want your children to be mediocre?

Of course not! You want your kids to succeed! In particular, you want your children to have a personal relationship with Jesus, marry the right person, and pursue their purpose in life with excellence. That is a pretty good start, isn't it? Truett Cathy, founder of Chick-fil-A, refers to those big three parenting priorities as Master, Mate, and Mission. If you lead your kids to spiritual truth, equip them to select the right marriage partner, and encourage them to pursue and live their dream, then you've certainly used your time wisely. In short, you want your children to become everything they were created to become. And that is exactly what God wants for you as well.

Do parents encourage their children to strive for mediocrity? Do you hope your son or daughter grows up and gets an average job, tolerates an average marriage, and then raises average kids who perpetuate that same cycle for the next generation? I don't believe God makes "average." The dim light of an average life is something we inflict on ourselves. Sometimes we make things difficult that should not be difficult. We turn the simple into the complex and confuse not only ourselves but the people around us as well. Make no mistake: **Your heavenly Father wants you to succeed.**

We all have the standard, factory-installed desire to reach our full potential. Sometimes this longing is temporarily smothered by a lack of

Five criteria to help crystallize your unique definition of success

1
CONTROLLABLE
Make your definition within your control, not based on outside circumstances or other people.

2
MEASURABLE
Make your definition quantifiable so that you can hold yourself accountable.

3
PERPETUAL
Formulate your definition so that you can satisfy it on a daily basis.

4
PERSONAL
Choose your own definition; don't borrow one.

5
PRINCIPLE BASED
Establish your definition on absolute truths, not on subjective, timely, or situational values.

wisdom or a sequence of poor choices, but it is still there, waiting to be activated. Consider how we hope and pray for good things to happen in the lives of those we love. Consider how we always pray for ourselves and our circumstances to improve, never to deteriorate. This is our built-in drive for success, our drive to see the various aspects of our life advance. Have you ever prayed for your life to fall apart, a cherished relationship to end, or a dear friend to become ill? I would hope not! You are, after all, designed for success.

YOU ARE FREED TO SUCCEED!

Why do so many people struggle with the idea of success? Is it because they hardly ever hear their pastor preach a sermon about success? Unless the sermon is based on Matthew 5–7, commonly referred to as the Sermon on the Mount, in most churches we rarely hear teaching about biblical success. In the Sermon on the Mount, however, Jesus distills the spiritual principles that both precede and promote true success. Practicing these principles frees you to maximize your full potential and become everything God intended for you to become. After you finish *Success Is Not an Accident,* I encourage you to reread the Sermon on the Mount and contemplate how relevant and practical the sayings of Jesus really are. Unfortunately, these principles of success are often poorly presented or misrepresented in our day and age, leading some to conclude that "that success stuff just doesn't sound biblical." For example, are we supposed to set goals, or are we to take no thought for tomorrow? Are we supposed to build our confidence, or have no confidence in the flesh? Should we strive for greatness, or should we be content in all circumstances? Are we to improve our self-image, or should we deny ourselves? These apparent contradictions have paralyzed many Christians from maximizing their potential. However, upon deep examination, the notion that success is wrong or even contrary to biblical truth cannot be seriously defended.

Like much of the enemy's handiwork, the tainting and shunning of success has been gradual and subtle. Put a negative spin on success, paint success as unbiblical, scare Christians away—then Christian leadership will slowly dissolve in a society clearly in need of godly direction. What a clever scheme.

Success has been hijacked from the very people who believe in the original book of success—the Bible. Over time, the concept of success has been so polluted and distorted that bold, godly success appears to have atrophied. Its influence is hardly felt. Many well-intentioned believers appear to be running from the potential they were blessed with at birth. As a result, God-inspired men and women are having less and less effect on the America they built. Interestingly, over the last decade an entire movement and ministry has attempted to rebrand true success with the word *significance*. Is this really necessary? Are we that afraid of the word *success*? In my mind, and in the minds of my clients, authentic success requires significance. **Significance doesn't follow success. It is the sum and substance of success.**

While Christians have stepped back, the secular world has been setting the agenda through legislative bodies, school boards, and the politically correct establishments that regulate the guidelines believers and nonbelievers alike must follow.

A PERFECT SYSTEM

Fortunately, all the confusion surrounding success need not exist at all. God wants each and every one of us to succeed, provided that our definition of success is right. **God wants us to reach our potential and contribute to the world in tremendous ways.** Success in the general sense is God's way of sharing abundance. He uses your success to bless others while you benefit yourself. Success is a *multiplier,* not a divider, as the media often tend to represent. Authentic success spills over to benefit many more beyond the minority who accepted the risk of failure. When individual success is promoted, an entire society gets rewarded. When you act with integrity, your success will not harm others in the least. You and everyone else you know can become successful without anyone suffering harm, setbacks, or downturns. Only God could author such a perfect system!

Success is completely voluntary. You have permission. You have the green light to succeed. What is success for a Christian? Remember, obedience to the rules and teachings of the Bible is just the minimum daily requirement. It is the starting point, the foundational standard. **True success, on the other hand, is maximum service to God.** Your heavenly Father desires that you be fully, in every single respect, the person he created you to be. I encourage you to reach for more than a life of mere obedience and "good living." Instead, strive for an abundant life of success in the service of others. Are you getting out of life everything that God intends for you? Can you stand to be blessed above and beyond your wildest dreams? The Bible is full of those who are "more than conquerors," and none of us should be content to be mediocre.

Although you probably agree that maximum service to God is a great definition of success, it's a difficult concept by which to evaluate yourself. So, for the express purpose of this book, we'll use the highly effective working definition of true success that we use in The 1% Club: **Success is the deliberate, measurable pursuit of prayerfully chosen, written goals.**

Stated another way, you are a success once you have seriously begun your expedition to maximize your full potential. Success, then, is not a single destination—and consequently, you can never completely arrive. **Success is, instead, an intentional approach to life that ensures you are a faithful steward of your gifts and talents.** This approach compels you to grow and develop. It forces you to desert your comfort zone, chisel your character, and chase the dream that God has personally arranged for you. Better still, success is an approach to life that is completely under your control. It does not depend on the outer circumstances of your life but on the inner condition of your soul. So with the above definition in mind, are you successful right now?

Did you pray about your goals *before* you set them?

Have you put your goals *in writing* for accountability?

Have you taken *measurable action* toward your goals?

A different way of viewing success is as an emotion we all want to experience consistently. We may be successful in the eyes of others yet not feel so successful inside our own skin. Or we may feel successful but not be perceived that way by others. Most of us go through life borrowing someone else's definition of success rather than coming up with our own! Through repeated media exposure, we find it easy to begin using cultural success markers.

Are you experiencing success right now? If you are not, take some time to re-examine your concept of success. Where does your definition come from? Whose definition are you using? I found that distinguishing between the words *achievement, happiness,* and *success* was a helpful exercise in formulating my own definition. Consider these three questions:

Can you be a success without achieving anything?

Can you be a high achiever without being successful?

Can you be happy without also being a success?

How did you answer these questions? Of course, your answer depends on how you define success. Is your definition challenging, attainable, and anchored in biblical truth? Or do you require all areas of your life to be perfect before you allow yourself to experience the emotion of success? Be aware that a common tendency is to set an almost unreachable standard for success while simultaneously creating a standard for failure that is easy to meet. As a result, you may routinely feel a lot less successful than is necessary. When you create a definition of success that allows you to experience the emotion consistently, you are also developing an awareness of success. And this heightened consciousness tends to promote even more and greater success in the future. Success breeds success. The working definition I proposed earlier invites you to experience success on your journey to your final destination.

Now it's your turn. Take a moment and develop a first draft of your personal definition of success by completing the short sentence below.

You can expect to revise it several times before you get it just right. Yes, I promise that it is okay to write in this book.

I experience success in my life when I (or, if I) . . .

_____

_____

_____

Once you have your fresh, constructive definition of success, allow some time to internalize it and really believe in it. You have to buy into it to get it working for you. Remember, success is the ongoing, proactive process of making God's desires your desires, becoming today a little more like the person he engineered you to become. I believe you should consider yourself a success the instant you take measurable action toward a prayerfully chosen goal that you have placed in writing. As you will learn in lesson 3, God plus goals plus you is an unbeatable combination!

"Fair" Is a Fantasy

Another key step in striving for success is to get over expecting life to be fair. A level playing field is a self-indulgent and unproductive fantasy. In this world, it will never happen, nor should it. **Insisting on a level playing field disrupts your attention and distracts you from your ultimate objective.** Instead, as a high performer, you must deal with the reality of the present situation. You need to focus on reaching your goals rather than on the obstacles that stand in your way. This choice leads to accomplishment and progress, and it leads away from aggravation and alienation. Recognize that everyone has disadvantages, handicaps, weaknesses, and various other crosses to bear. A big part of life is learning how to transform your disadvantages into advantages. While directing your energy toward "making things fair" is often counterproductive, channeling your spiritual, mental, and physical energy toward achieving meaningful goals is a constructive investment of time.

Some people are naturally more intelligent than others. Some people are more creative than others. Some are born into poverty, and some into wealth. Some receive great love and little else, while many others are given everything but love. Some people are considered better looking than others. Some people can run faster, jump higher, or hit a baseball farther than others. Some receive the best of educations and contribute little to the world, while others get little formal education yet leave a magnificent mark. Some have fast metabolisms while others must exercise twice as much just to keep pace. Some people are predisposed to migraines and sinus infections and others are not . . . and so on. This phenomenon is called life.

The truth is that life, if viewed as a card game, deals good hands, bad hands, and average hands. And whichever hand you receive, you must play! You can win with any hand, and you can lose with any hand. It's totally up to you how you play the game! Life is filled with champions who drew extremely poor hands and losers who drew terrific hands. **In life, you will never be dealt a hand that, with God's help, cannot be turned into a winning one.** Success is for you and for anyone willing to take the initiative and pay the price. If you put into practice the principles outlined in each lesson of this book, you will be well equipped to do whatever it takes to turn your hand into a winner! Go for it!

SOW, THEN REAP

Success is a planned outcome, not an accident. Success and mediocrity are both absolutely predictable because they follow the natural and immutable law of sowing and reaping. Simply stated, if you want to reap more rewards, you must sow more service, contribution, and value. That is the no-nonsense formula. Some of God's blessings have prerequisites! Success in life is not based on need but on seed. So you've got to become good at either planting in the springtime or begging in the fall.

The Bible says, "Do not be deceived, God is not mocked; for whatever a man sows, that he will also reap" (Galatians 6:7, NKJV). Unfortunately, many Americans have been misled into believing they will not be held accountable for their choices and that they will miraculously harvest something other than what they planted. I call this the Big Lie. This dangerously popular distortion promotes mediocrity and underachievement. Consider the effort and expense Americans undertake to cure diseases and social problems while they do very little, if anything, to avoid them. It is popular today to treat the symptom of a problem, but it is often considered insensitive or intolerant to address the root causes. As a result, our society denies that effects really do have causes.

The truth is this: There are no exceptions to the law of causality. It is impartial and impersonal, and it comes to us in a particular order—first sow, then reap. This God-given natural law was old when the pyramids were new. Like gravity, it works twenty-four hours a day, seven days a week, everywhere in the world, regardless of whether anyone has ever told you about it or whether you consider it to be fair. It is simply impossible to harvest something that has not been sown, though many squander their entire lives attempting to do just this, only to end up frustrated.

> **When you try to get something for nothing, you become nothing.**

Success is the effect generated by right thinking and right actions. Success and failure are not accidents but consequences. **If you want to know what you sowed in the past, look around you and see what you are reaping today.** You begin your climb toward your full potential as a human being the moment you accept the truth that cause and consequence are inseparable.

The mark of a spiritually mature, mentally healthy individual is accepting complete responsibility for one's life. When you accept total responsibility, you recognize that you are the cause of all your choices, decisions, and actions. When you are anchored in the reality of responsibility, you are far more likely to act in ways that will not later become causes of regret, frustration, or embarrassment.

EVERYTHING COUNTS

Life offers all of us a special deal indefinitely. With every choice, we receive at least one free consequence. Everything you do or fail to do counts. Every action has a consequence, even if it isn't immediate. At

What are the likely consequences of each of these actions?

- jumping off a building

- doing aerobic exercise daily

- watching two or more hours of TV every day

- reading for one hour each day

- sitting in the sun without sunscreen

- investing 10 percent of your income

- using illicit drugs

- eating a diet of whole grains and fresh fruits and vegetables

- eating fried foods

- running in front of a speeding truck

- robbing a bank

- lying to your best friend

- studying hard in school

- smoking

- writing down goals

- drinking excessive alcohol

- drinking just a little alcohol

- drinking no alcohol

- studying parenting

- reading a book on marriage

- touching a hot stove

- studying successful people

- praying

- purchasing depreciating assets

- spending beyond your means

- waking up at 5 a.m.

- waking up at 7 a.m.

Remember, when you make a choice, you also choose the consequence of that choice.

this moment, you are either becoming more like the person God wants you to become, or you are not! There is no neutrality.

A number of years ago I was watching a baseball game on TV. The base runner, Deion Sanders, attempted to steal second base but came up about two feet short from the bag as he slid. He immediately sprang to his feet and backtracked toward first base. Seconds later, when it became inevitable that he was going to be tagged out, Sanders put his hands together in the football time-out sign. He yelled, "Time-out, time-out!"—to no avail, but to laughter from the fielder and the umpire. Sanders was tagged out. That is the way life is. Whether you're running the bases or pursuing your goals, there are no time-outs. The sooner you learn and apply this lesson, the better.

Nobody can stop the ticking clock. If you try to call time-out, you will always be tagged out. What you do Friday night counts, just as what you do Sunday morning or Thursday afternoon counts. An extraordinary life is simply the accumulation of thousands of efforts, often unseen by others, that lead to the accomplishment of worthwhile goals. **You are rich with choice, and your choices reveal who you really are.** More than any other single factor, you are where you are today because of the choices you have made. You've made decisions about what to learn and what not to learn. You have made decisions about who to spend your time with. You've made decisions to believe some things and not to believe others. You've made, or will have to make, decisions about whom you will date, whom you will marry, and whether you will have children. You've chosen to persevere or chosen to give up. You've made decisions on whether or not you will drink, smoke, or use drugs. You have chosen what you will eat or not eat. You've decided either to write down exciting goals for your life or just to wing it. You have made decisions to give in to fear as well as decisions to press on in the face of fear. You have decided to be the best and at other times decided to act like all the rest.

Consider for a moment all the decisions you've made in the last three years or even in just the last twelve months. These choices are made daily, hourly, and minute by minute. Imagine having made a different choice in some key area. How might your professional life be different?

How might your marriage be different? How might your health and energy be different? Give this some thoughtful reflection. **How might your life be different today with a handful of different choices?**

Let me encourage you to do something differently now: Make today the turning point. Whether it's your career or your home life, your fitness or your faith, you can start making wiser decisions and taking different steps today. Sooner than you may think possible, you will find yourself in a much better place than where you are right now.

What's Your Excuse?

I believe the slogan of the Paralympics says it all: "What's your excuse?" Questions are often the best teachers because they prompt us to think through an issue. When we're told something, we're likely to smile politely and then let our thoughts drift to another subject. Questions can be captivating because we're conditioned to answer them. So ask yourself,

"What is my excuse?" What images does this question evoke in your mind? As I ask myself, "What is my excuse?" my mind races to the

My father taught me that the only helping hand you're ever going to be able to rely on is at the end of your sleeve.
—J. C. Watts

aspects of my life that aren't quite as I want them to be. The question reminds me of the excuses I've given others and those I've silently told myself. It makes me laugh a little at myself and reminds me that while I was making excuses, others just like me were making progress.

I remember the first time I heard the classic excuse "My dog ate my homework" from a third-grade classmate who didn't even have a dog. The entire class, including the teacher, broke out in laughter. I don't remember whether the excuse was effective, but I do remember the laughter and the embarrassed expression on my classmate's face. Looking back, I realize how appropriate the laughter was. Excuses should be laughed at, not dignified. Excuses and responsibility cannot coexist. It's very easy to say, "I'm not responsible," and so hard to say, "I am responsible." If there is anything in your life that is not the way you want it to be, you and only you are responsible for changing it. You must believe that it is up to you to create solutions to the challenges of life. Whether they are big or small, you're still responsible. Each time you give an excuse, you diminish your respect, your credibility, and your integrity. Each time you make an excuse, you reinforce your propensity to make even more excuses in the future, and excuse making becomes a habit. The irresponsible person believes finding the solutions to the problems of life is someone else's department.

Whenever you act irresponsibly and feel the need to make excuses, your brain goes into overdrive, attempting to rationalize your lack of results. Unless you make a commitment to the choice of excuse-free living, you will always be able to find excuses.

THE EXCUSE-FREE ZONE

Commit to making your home, car, and office excuse-free zones. If a situation arises in which previously you would have made an excuse, substitute the words, "I am responsible." Look only to yourself for the cause of your problems. If you are not happy with an aspect of your life, accept that you are responsible for it. Either you passively allowed it to happen or you actively created it. This is not an invitation to beat up on yourself but an encouragement to see the truth of how and why you got to where you are. Only when you acknowledge the truth can you be freed to build a future that is far more attractive than the past.

Whenever something doesn't work out the way you hoped, claim responsibility and ask yourself, "What could I have done to avoid the problem?" Imagine opening your refrigerator and taking out the orange juice. Following the instructions on the label, you begin to shake the carton vigorously—only to have the cap fly off and orange juice spew all over you, the counters, the floor, and even a little on the ceiling. At this point, you have two options:

1. You can immediately blame the numskull who didn't screw on the cap after he used it and demand that he help you clean up, or . . .

2. You can remind yourself, "This mess could have been avoided altogether if I had only checked the cap before I started shaking the carton.

The Excuse Exploder

Whenever you think of an excuse, ask yourself if there has ever been anyone in similar circumstances who succeeded in spite of them. When you move beyond the whining and justifying, you'll find that the answer is almost always yes. Somebody somewhere has usually had it far worse than you and still succeeded. And the moment you want a goal more than you want an excuse, you can succeed as well. Refuse to appoint yourself a victim. Victims don't have to take action; they're too busy dwelling on injustice and being bitter. Remember, you will always be able to come up with an eloquent excuse, but no excuse has a shelf life of more than twenty-four hours.

Of course, it would have been nice if the previous person had secured the cap, but the power to prevent this situation was in my hands."

Taking responsibility for your life is like being a good, defensive driver. If your car is totaled in an accident, you can't take much comfort from the fact that you had the green light. Blaming the other driver won't help much either; it will only defer your attention from what you need to learn. The question that will resonate in your mind is, "What could I have done to prevent this?" Stay empowered and in control by analyzing all unpleasant situations from the perspective of what *you* can do to avoid their recurrence in the future.

Excuses are contagious, self-defeating bad habits. Where you find one person making an excuse, you'll find others infected with "excusitis" as well. You don't like to hear excuses from other people, and they don't like to hear yours either! Stop excuses before they start by creating an environment conducive to success. Make it easy for yourself and others you depend on to succeed by anticipating and eliminating all excuses in advance. This is the true measure of how intensely you desire your goal.

The only thing more damaging to your success than making an excuse is making the same excuse twice. Remember, there is never enough room for both buts and brilliance. You must make the choice. Do I want my "Yeah, but," or do I want my goal?

Feelers and Doers

The world can be divided into two kinds of people: feelers and doers. Feelers take initiative only when they feel like doing so. In other words, they feel their way into action. If something makes sense at the moment, is convenient, is justified, or is just easy, then they do it. If they don't feel like doing something that will advance their goals, they won't do it. If a feeler feels like exercising, he will. If he doesn't feel like exercising, he won't. If a feeler feels like doing her daily devotions, she will. But if she feels like sleeping in instead, she will sleep late. If a feeler feels like nurturing his marriage relationship, he will. If not, he won't. His decision-making ability is wired to his short-term emotional appetite. He is a prisoner of the desire for instant gratification, and he will suffer the long-term consequences of this short-term perspective. Feeling-driven thinking, as popular as it is in our culture today, is shallow thinking. It signals weak character, lack of conviction, and spiritual immaturity. Fortunately, feeling-driven thinking is just an unproductive habit that can be changed.

Doers, on the other hand, act their way into feeling. After determining what needs to be

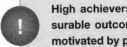

High achievers are motivated by pleasurable outcomes. Underachievers are motivated by pleasurable methods.

done based on their goals, doers take action. They just do it. If they don't feel like taking action, they consider that emotion a distraction and take action in spite of it. They refuse to let their craving for short-term comfort divert them from their long-term goal and the blessings that go along with it.

You become a doer by making a deliberate decision to do so. You become a feeler by default, by neglecting to consider this aspect of your character at all. In the absence of a decision to do otherwise, we are all prone to giving in to the worst side of human nature. We are all likely to engage in actions that produce only immediate payback.

The alternative to a life restricted by our feelings is an unlimited life characterized by deliberate and decisive action. The antidote to a safe life of comfort and mediocrity is a bold life of character and courage. You can train yourself to live a life of action by shifting your thinking from short-term to long-term. This means you must consider the long-term ramifications of every action you take. Ask, "If this act were to turn into a habit for me, would that be in my best long-term interests?" If the answer is no, then don't do it. When faced with an important decision, ask yourself, "In light of where I've been, where I am today, and who I intend to become in the future, what is the wise thing to do in this situation?" Even simpler, you could ask, "What's my goal, and will this clearly move me in the direction of my goal?" Or, "How might this decision affect me twenty years from now?" Another question is, "How might this decision affect me one thousand years from now?" That one should get you thinking! Remember, feelings come and go, but consequences last forever.

The quality of our decisions is determined first and foremost by our perspective, or frame of reference. If our time horizon is long, then we will likely reap the effects of wise choices. If our horizon is short, then we will inevitably suffer the negative consequences that correspond with short-term thinking.

Abundance or Survival?

You can walk up to the ocean of abundance with a thimble or a tanker truck. Unfortunately, most people choose the thimble, never knowing that there is an alternative. Remind yourself that **God is the infinite source and ultimate provider of all good things.** Our heavenly Father has poured an inexhaustible supply of abundance onto this earth, ready for us to multiply it even further if we are willing to take the initiative. Most people do not seize the initiative simply because they have learned to think in terms of survival rather than in terms of plenty. This attitude is often referred to as a scarcity mentality and is inherently pessimistic. People with a scarcity mind-set are excessively aware of what they *do not* want in life and hesitant about what they *do* want. They have long mental lists of why things can't be done and why it is of no use to even try. "Why set a goal when you cannot possibly achieve it?" is a typical response of these deficit thinkers. A scarcity or poverty mentality sends one into survival mode, where just getting by becomes the goal and, consequently, the ceiling. Of course, those suffering from this stagnant outlook are seldom aware of it.

An abundance consciousness, on the other hand, is anchored in faith, possibilities, and huge thinking. In this state, we concentrate on how and why things can be done. An abundance thinker dwells on the opportunities that exist now as well as those that should exist. An *abundance* mentality precedes all extraordinary accomplishment, and it is your birthright. Get away from what is *realistic* and consider the seemingly impossible possibilities. Stop asking what a good goal would be and start asking God what your most magnificent goal should and could be.

The Bill of Responsibilities

I.   You have the responsibility to ask only for opportunity.

II. You have the responsibility to seek and find your true place in life.

III. You have the responsibility to write down compelling goals for your life.

IV. You have the responsibility to invest your minutes and hours wisely.

V.   You have the responsibility to visualize the attainment of your goals in rich, vivid detail.

VI. You have the responsibility to talk yourself into success.

VII. You have the responsibility to choose a high-energy lifestyle.

VIII. You have the responsibility to develop every area of your life to its maximum.

IX. You have the responsibility to provide more value and contribution if you desire more rewards.

X.   You have the responsibility to persist until you succeed.

No matter how prosperous your mind-set is, it can be even more prosperous. **Remember, your success blesses others.** As you increase the quality and quantity of your service to others, your rewards increase as a natural consequence. As you become more abundant in your thinking, you become like a formerly color-blind child in a fabulous garden, suddenly able to see the rich images that have been there all along. You can tune in to scarcity, or you can tune in to abundance. Again, it is your choice. When you take responsibility for your actions, accept that life isn't fair, get rid of excuses, become a doer, and develop an abundance mentality, you will break down many of the barriers keeping you from true success. You will be well on the way to maximizing the potential that God has given you.

Lesson 1 Questions for Reflection

What does success mean to you? Are you successful now? Do you feel successful? How do you define true success?

What is mediocrity? What examples of it have you witnessed recently? How do you prevent mediocrity from attacking you, your family, or your business?

What messages about success are promoted in our culture through the media, political leaders, churches, school curricula, and so forth, and how do they shape your thinking?

Who in your life would most benefit if you raised your standards and demanded far more from yourself?

Describe your life and passions ten years ago. What was your focus? What were your challenges? What were your hopes and dreams?

Whom can you influence with the ideas from this lesson in the next forty-eight hours?

LESSON 1 ASSIGNMENTS

1 | Write out your personal definitions of success and mediocrity.

2 | Draw a line down the center of a piece of paper. On the left-hand side, write down everything in your life that you can control, either partially or completely. Label this column "God and Me." In the right-hand column, write down those aspects of your life over which you have absolutely no control. You can label this column "Let God."

3 | Write out ten of your strengths or positive traits.

4 | Write out ten of your past accomplishments, big or small.

5 | Write out ten of your greatest blessings to date.

6 | Write out ten blessings you expect to be grateful for nine years from now.

7 | Describe your ideal day nine years in the future. Begin with the moment you wake up and follow through until you drift off to sleep, and include as many emotion-provoking details as possible.

Choose Who You Want to Become

If you want your purpose in life to become a magnificent obsession, you must develop and constantly review your personal mission statement.

In this lesson, you will learn to

- Recognize your true identity
- Choose who you want to become
- Cultivate the passion of personal mission
- Live more honestly, freely, and intuitively
- Craft an inspiring personal mission statement
- Align your goals with your purpose

Now that you have a working definition of success and understand that God wants you to succeed, I want you to get on fire about the prospect of maximizing your potential. Get passionate! You were created in the image and likeness of God to do wise, wonderful, and grand things with the limited time you have here on earth. So why not dare to do magnificent things with, through, and for God? After all, how does thinking small serve the world? Accept the burden and blessing of success. Do you really believe that all the vast plans of God have already been accomplished? Have the greatest lives already been lived? Have the greatest marriages already happened? Have the best books and songs already been written? Have the best inventions already been created? Have the best sermons already been delivered? Are the greatest high-tech breakthroughs behind us? Have the ultimate medical advances already occurred? Have the most creative businesses already been launched? The best of everything may, in fact, be yet to come. Today or tomorrow may very well be the most electrifying day of history.

In this lesson, I am going to challenge you to consider and clarify your life's purpose. We will also discuss uncovering what I call your Genius and the role it plays in helping you understand your purpose. Even more important, your Genius helps you live each day with a greater sense of mission, with a greater sense of enthusiasm, and with a real hunger to make a significant, positive difference with your life.

Who Are You Now?

You are a beautiful, wonderful child of God! This is the truth, whether or not you know it or believe it. Pause for a moment and marvel at what this must mean. Think about yourself as a child of God, one of the family, a kid of the King. You are an original masterpiece. Your DNA proves it. There has never been anyone just like you, and there never will be anyone just like you. God has not made anyone else out of better clay than he has made you. It's critical to remember your true identity. When you perceive yourself as a child of God, you will not see restrictions on the amount of impact you can have in this world. How you see yourself on the inside sets the ceiling for what God can do with you on the outside. Your life here on earth is your special, unrepeatable opportunity to magnify the greatness God has placed within you.

Who Are You Becoming?

Before you choose your goals, it is wise to first choose who you want to become. This means deciding in advance how you believe God wants you to change. As human beings, we need a sense of purpose in our lives as much as we need food, water, and oxygen. This sense of purpose provides meaning and significance. It makes us feel useful and is a constant reminder that our life matters. When you have a deep sense of purpose or mission, you live from the inside out. This means *who* you are triggers *what* you do. Your outer life accurately reflects your values, priorities, and principles. You begin living more authentically, more freely, and more intuitively. When

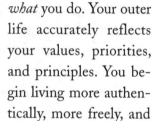

Today will take its place as a single tile in the mosaic of our finished lives—to either add to its beauty and harmony or detract from it in an undedicated, purposeless life. *—Earl Nightingale*

you tap into the wellspring of your personal mission, you become more creative, energetic, and passionate. You become totally absorbed in the pursuit of your goals, like a child at play, because your goals are in sync with what you are all about.

Without a deep sense of purpose, life is devoid of true significance or long-term meaning. This type of existence is characterized by going through the motions, cynicism, pessimism, apathy, and ultimately a life of mediocrity. It is living perpetually in survival mode. It's a life that constantly needs to be filled up with things from the outside—busyness, distractions, and continuous activity.

You have no greater responsibility than to determine what God put you here on earth to accomplish. Why do you exist? Generally, everyone shares the common purposes of learning, growing, and contributing, but what about you specifically? How do you believe God wants the world to be different because of your particular life?

YOUR TRUE PLACE

You may not have uncovered it yet, but there is undoubtedly an answer to that question. It is worth searching for, because the answer reveals your purpose. And in this purpose you must find your true place, or what we in The 1% Club call your Genius. **Your true place is your unique path to glorifying God.** When you arrive in your true place, you will know it. You will feel a sense of destiny as what you most love to do merges with what you do best. This is where you will spend your life in your own way, making the difference that you are uniquely equipped to make. The more you experience your true place, the more you will be drawn to it. The tinge of dissatisfaction, which perhaps only you knew existed, will disappear. You will enjoy invigorating surges of self-worth, as there will no longer be a need to compare yourself with anyone else. You will be healthier, more prosperous, and full of joy.

While each of us has many areas where we can do well, there is but one Genius. God had one particular thing in mind when he made you.

WHAT'S YOUR DREAM?

You might initially recognize this one particular thing as your ultimate vision or dream. For some, this dream will shake the entire world. For others, it will soothe just one tiny home. In either case, the world will be left a better place.

Sooner or later, we are all confronted with the question of whether we are living on purpose—whether or not we are heeding our call and following our ultimate vision. No matter how far you may have strayed from your true place, you can always find it again. Your true place is always waiting for you because

 Do what you love, and you'll stop being your own worst enemy.

no one but you can fill it. That's a great thought! So take comfort in knowing that every experience you have ever had, no matter how seemingly unrelated, can be used to your advantage in your true place when you finally find it. And you will find it . . . if you will wholeheartedly look for it.

Are you now serving God by becoming each day a little more like the person he wants you to become? Your purpose is not something to achieve; rather, it is something to be satisfied and quenched. So who are you becoming here on earth? Throughout your life, you will be changing constantly and becoming someone new, either slightly or extensively different from the previous version of yourself. With each change, you will either move closer to your true place or move further away.

For most people, change just happens. Change is considered an external event that occurs randomly and haphazardly. Most people allow themselves to be molded and thrown off course by their circumstances. But as James Allen writes in his book *As a Man Thinketh*, "Circumstance does not make a man, it reveals him."[1] This is a critical principle of human nature.

OUR PRIVATE THOUGHTS

Our circumstances are just a reflection of what is going on inside our secret world of thoughts, emotions, and beliefs. What we think about most will ultimately be revealed for everyone to see. In other words, our private thoughts don't stay private for very long. Human beings are really "human becomings." As we begin to renew our thinking, our world changes with us. As we become better, our lives become better. The prerequisite for changing circumstances is that you must first change yourself. To have it any other way is like pretending the tail can wag the dog. Living on purpose requires deliberately deciding in advance how you are going to grow more like the person God wants you to become. This decision requires that you get in touch with your core desires. It is these high-intensity desires, sometimes called the DNA of success, that reveal what role God made you to fill. Later in this lesson, I'll share some clues that will help you identify your Genius.

I believe that God's will for you is something wonderful and glorious—far better than anything you could ever design for yourself. So don't conform to the average life. Fight off this pull of mediocrity and stand out! Be unconventional. Be an original. Refuse to let yourself be a common copy. Accept that you have been custom-made by God to serve an exclusive function in this world, even if that role and a plan to fulfill it are not yet clear to you. This is your true place—and it's up to you to find it. There are no extra human beings. God has a plan and a place for everyone, and that includes you.

IS EVERYONE DOING IT?

So if God's will is so compelling, why isn't everyone doing it? After working with thousands of ambitious clients over the last sixteen years and undertaking an enormous amount of personal research, I've developed some strong conclusions about how our talents, our mission, and God's will are intertwined:

- God has a particular objective for your life. I've touched a bit on this already.

- This objective (or purpose for your life) coincides with your gifts and talents and a host of other heavenly factors.

- Your areas of interest—the activities and pursuits that you find most enjoyable and attractive—are the best indicators of strong talent and giftedness.

When you engage in activities that demand your special talent, your brain releases chemicals that trigger satisfaction as an incentive for you to continue in this area. It is a positive reinforcement mechanism that is all part of God's perfect design. These talents then get converted into strengths and eventually into Genius if we sustain the course long enough.

Our unique conglomeration of character, talents, life experiences, and personality merge and spark a dream within each of us. The more often we engage in our strengths, the more crystallized our ultimate vision becomes.

With this God-given dream imprinted on our minds, we become intrinsically motivated, needing less and less prodding from the outside. We become inwardly directed, and self-discipline comes virtually without effort.

This whole process is countercultural. Instead of competing to max out their God-given potential, most people in our society compete to keep up with one another. They are in the wrong race. Philosophically, they tend to desire comfort more than character. Strategically, they often find themselves in the wrong career. Tactically, they've resigned themselves to simply enjoying their evenings, weekends, and vacations, with no long-term goals. Most people underperform because they were sloppy in choosing the right race for themselves in the first place. With three kids, a second home, and twenty years spent in their current field, many people feel trapped.

The dream God plants in your heart, in your DNA, will not come to fruition by accident. Naturally, there is a price. In a nutshell, the price requires that you surrender the concepts of safety, security, and comfort in exchange for the higher rewards of living the life God gave *you* and leaving your unmistakable mark on the world. You must grant yourself a promotion and escape from your personal comfort zone if you want to become the difference maker that you were designed to become. Jump, and the net will appear!

All along the path, you will face resistance—institutional, cultural, relational, financial, and mental. This is simply part of the dream game. You must press on in the face of all the pressure to conform. You must take action that leaves no doubt you are committed to your ultimate vision—and you must do this before you have the money, before you have the confidence, and even before you have the blessing of those closest to you. You must first commit unconditionally, then the plan will come and the resources will emerge. Only after you give up all thought of retreat will you become an unstoppable force.

Persistently ask God these three questions: *Who am I? Why am I here? Where do you want me to go?* Ask God to reveal his will for you through your desires.

EXCELLENCE IS INEVITABLE!

Now let's move a little deeper into the concept of Genius, and in particular, how it applies to your work. **Your area of Genius is the specific**

point where what you enjoy doing most intersects with what you do best. This is where you are capable of making the greatest contribution in the world. Excellence is inevitable once you find this Genius.

How do you find your Genius? First, determine what you naturally enjoy. Ask yourself what you'd do all day long if money were not a factor. Only when you really love what you do as much as a cherished hobby will you have what it takes to generate tremendous results. A Genius is someone who believes in the ideas that God sends and then takes action.

What is God whispering in your ear? What do you secretly want to do with your life? Exercise the courage to honestly identify where you have been uniquely blessed—where you have special talents and abilities. If you don't know, pray about it. Ask your spouse. Ask your friends. But seek it out. I believe you have the ability to become outstanding in at least one thing if you are selective and if you throw your whole heart into becoming the best. You must give up all hope of becoming excellent—and enjoying the abundant opportunities that come with it—if you can't lose yourself with enthusiasm for what you do. As the old saying goes, "Do what you love—love what you do." Start thanking God it's Monday!

GENIUS IS AS GENIUS DOES

I have been emphasizing the concept of Genius, which is the ability to focus on your unique strength to the exclusion of all else. This is accomplished by identifying your Genius and then over a period of years eliminating all those activities that interfere with it or oppose it. The concept of Genius is closely aligned with two major principles of peak personal performance:

- The Strength Principle, which is that by focusing on your strengths, you ultimately render your weaknesses irrelevant

- The 80/20 Principle, which is that 80 percent of your results come from only 20 percent of your inputs

Let's examine this by more closely defining your Genius. We're not talking about Einstein genius; we're talking about entrepreneurial or performance genius. Sometimes I call it Forrest Gump genius, meaning it's a way of acting. To paraphrase Forrest's mother, "Genius is as Genius does." Your Genius is a set of related activities that collectively produce superior rewards in the marketplace. Whether you're a star athlete, a pastor, a business leader, an FBI agent, an entrepreneur, a stay-at-home parent, or a teacher, you have a marketplace—a group of people you are charged with serving. When you operate in your Genius, you produce outstanding results. Best of all, these outcomes are generated with a disproportionately small but extremely calculated investment of time and effort.

Your Genius is where you are most fully leveraged. You can achieve far more with less time, effort, and energy. In many fields, this means you will be able to work less and earn even more by significantly increasing the dollar value of each hour of your time. For others, you will simply be much more productive. By operating within your Genius, you can do less but become much more. Your Genius is where you're capable of making the greatest difference in the world.

Almost everyone has experienced brief glimpses of Genius, yet only a small minority have capitalized on their latent potential and transformed it into their daily operating system. Here are seven clues that will help you identify your Genius.

Passion. Your area of Genius will always be characterized by enthusiasm, intense interest, and pure fun. This passion will be difficult to turn off, even when you're away from work. You'll have boundless energy; working in your area of Genius will energize you physically, mentally, and emotionally. When you do experience fatigue, it will be accompanied by a powerful sense of satisfaction.

Rapid and Continuous Learning. In your area of Genius, you'll notice that learning new information takes little time. New concepts are easily visualized and quickly integrated into your existing knowledge base. Just as important, the learning process is fun, and never-ending improvement comes naturally.

Strong Memory. Your area of Genius is characterized by a vivid, clear, almost perfect memory. Facts, figures, dates, names, conversations, and key points related to your Genius activities are effortlessly recalled when needed.

Flow. When you're operating in your Genius, you'll tend to get totally immersed in what you're doing. World-class athletes sometimes refer to being "in the zone" when they're totally absorbed in the present moment and able to shut out everything else.

Using Intuition. In your Genius, you'll naturally tap into and be inclined to follow your intuitive hunches, and most importantly, you will be right. Expect to experience a strong, instinctual knowing that helps you make quick, positive decisions to move you toward your goal.

Absence of Burnout. By operating in your Genius, you will insulate yourself from burnout. Since you'll be doing what you do best and most love to do, you will get more done in less time and be happier, healthier, and much more balanced. Burnout is the mental, emotional, and physical consequence of overwork in an area of weakness or non-Genius. Burnout is the breaking-point result of accumulated resistance to non-Genius activity.

Yearning. When you experience a deep desire that just won't go away, it's a strong sign that you may be approaching your Genius. Several summers ago, one of my sons kept holding a ball underneath the water in the hot tub. When he released it, it would shoot like a rocket to the surface and up into the air. He seemed to get a kick out of this process, especially when the ball smacked his dad in the face. No matter how deep he held the ball or how often he repeated this exercise, the ball still shot up to the surface. And this is exactly how a yearning works. No matter how often or how deeply you try to bury it, it will keep emerging until you do something about it. Your Genius is longing to be released once and for all.

The "Wing-It" Factor. Have you ever attempted something, completed it with very little effort or preparation, and then received tremendous feedback and praise? This means you "winged it" and got away with it. This can be a great clue to your Genius. If you have the talent to wing it and get great results, how well could you do with a little more prepara-tion? How well could you do with a lot more practice? One of the biggest performance mistakes people make is continuing to wing it because they can, rather than investing the effort and time to make it to the top one percent. Where do you still wing it? It's worth thinking about.

Your Personal Mission Statement

In this next segment, I want to coach you through the process of creat-ing your personal mission statement. I will share with you an exercise I assign to my 1% Club clients as they develop their personal missions, and I will give you a simple recipe that will help you generate the first draft.

A personal mission statement is a written articulation of your God-given potential—as God sees it. It expresses your unique purpose for living. Your personal mission statement encourages you to change in a deliberate, preconceived direction. The process of constructing the state-ment forces you to think seriously about the vital areas of your life and to clarify your long-term direction. Creating a personal mission statement requires reflection, introspection, and considerable mental effort. For this reason, it is not an exercise that is appealing to everyone.

A POWERFUL EXERCISE

A mission statement is a written, present-tense articulation of exactly what type of person you believe God wants you to become. More im-portantly, it states what you are willing to do differently in the present to become that person in the future. A good mission statement clarifies what is allowable in your life. It helps you say "yes" to the right things and "no way" to the wrong things. It reminds you of what is true and false. It is a bridge from intention to action, an outward sign that you have accepted complete responsibility for your life. Here's a sample to get your creative juices flowing:

My Mission

My mission is to set an excellent example by massively contributing and serving others while I am continuously learning, growing, and improving myself, all to the glory of God. I am a child of God. I obey God's commandments and reap the natural benefits. I confidently claim the glorious and wonderful promises that my heavenly Father has made to me. I am grateful to God for each new day and the opportunity to begin a new . . .

I experience and enjoy perfect health! Developing my full potential and living consistently with my values is not possible without being in excellent physical condition. My diet is filled with life-enhancing foods. I exercise aerobically, take the necessary time to relax, sleep, and practice deep breathing. I have trained my mind to focus on my goals and . . .

I am a loving, loyal, and fun marriage partner. I take sufficient and meaningful time with my spouse, helping and encouraging him or her in the areas of spiritual, mental, social, professional, and financial growth . . .

I am a loving, wise, and fun parent. I develop strong family unity. I take all the training and education in child rearing I can get so that I am always improving as a parent. I understand that my actions and habits as a parent speak much louder than my words . . .

I am a master of my profession. I look for and find opportunities, always making things happen. My clients trust me, appreciate me, and seek my counsel without hesitation. I plan my time wisely each year, each quarter, each week, and every morning—and then I work my plan. I love my career, and its rich rewards are a blessing to my family . . .

I am a super-learning machine! I am committed to constant personal and professional development. I learn from those who have gone before me and . . .

To study some additional sample mission statements, please visit
www.1percentclub.com/missionstatements.

When you have completed your mission statement, you will have a clear picture of the person you hope to become, which dramatically increases the odds that you will actually become that person. Your mission statement will be the unifying element around which you organize the rest of your life. And if you want your mission in life to become a magnificent obsession, you have to constantly remind yourself of that mission. If you review your mission statement regularly, it will hold you accountable to changing and improving in a deliberate, preconceived direction. As you travel down the path of discovering your Genius and finding your life's purpose, always remember that your success blesses others!

Lesson 2 Questions for Reflection

If money were not a consideration—if you were taken care of financially and could use your days any way you wanted to—how would you spend most of your time?

What is the most important piece of career advice you would pass on to your child?

In what aspects of your life do other people tend to be most impressed with your performance?

What were four specific activities you loved doing when you were ten years old?

What recurring activities cause you to feel distracted or "off purpose"?

———————— ∞ ————————

Whom can you influence with the ideas from this lesson in the next forty-eight hours?

The Personal Mission Statement Worksheet

1 | What three qualities would you most like to have associated with your reputation?

A.

B.

C.

2 | What three activities do you find most enjoyable?

A.

B.

C.

3 | What three activities are most important to you?

A.

B.

C.

4 | What three things would you like to change about life if you had no restrictions or limitations?

A.

B.

C.

5 | What six things do you want in life more than anything else? Be limitless in your thinking.

A.	D.
B.	E.
C.	F.

6 | Who are the three people you admire most and why?

A.

B.

C.

The Personal Mission Statement Worksheet

7 | Of the people you admire most, what one quality do they all have in common?

8 | What would you be willing to die for if you had to?

9 | Why do you go to work in the morning?

10 | What are your four most important roles in life *(friend, salesperson, entrepreneur, student, uncle, husband, mother, etc.)*?

A.   C.

B.   D.

11 | What qualities would you like to be known for in each of these roles? *(For examples, see pages 48–49.)*

A.   C.

B.   D.

12 | What evidence would prove you have those qualities?

The Personal Mission Statement Worksheet

13 | Which three metaphors accurately describe your outlook on life? Why?

- Life is a game.
- Life is a bowl of cherries.
- Life is the pits.
- Life is a test.
- Life is a competition.
- Life is a gift.
- Life is a dance.
- Life is like a movie.
- Life is a cycle of seasons.
- Life is a struggle.
- Life is like a school.
- Life is a challenge.
- Life is a sprint.
- Life is a marathon.
- Life is a gamble.

14 | What would you like to see written on your tombstone?

15 | If you could write your own eulogy, what would you want it to say?

The Personal Mission Statement Outline

1 | Statement of purpose *(one sentence, in twenty-five words or less):*
My mission is to . . .

On your Personal Mission Statement Worksheet, you identified four roles *(see questions 10–12)*. Answer the following questions for each role:

2 | Role A

a. Qualities/Description *(1–2 sentences)*
I am . . .

b. Evidence, Actions, Responsibilities *(1–2 sentences)*
I . . .

3 | Role B

a. Qualities/Description *(1–2 sentences)*

b. Evidence, Actions, Responsibilities *(1–2 sentences)*

4 | Role C

a. Qualities/Description *(1–2 sentences)*

b. Evidence, Actions, Responsibilities *(1–2 sentences)*

5 | Role D

a. Qualities/Description *(1–2 sentences)*

b. Evidence, Actions, Responsibilities *(1–2 sentences)*

6 | Summary and Conclusion *(3–5 sentences)*

My personal philosophy of life and success *(see lesson 1):*

LESSON 2 ASSIGNMENT

Using the outline provided on page 46, compose the first draft of your personal mission statement. Make sure it is written in present tense as if it were true today.

Ideal Qualities

accepting	responsible	considerate
dynamic	genuine	optimistic
exceptional	humorous	unpretentious
confident	rational	tolerant
daring	charming	attractive
intuitive	passionate	sociable
motivated	smart	good natured
gentle	expressive	adept
humble	skillful	encouraging
quick	thoughtful	stimulating
responsive	attentive	perceptive
patient	open minded	dependable
precise	conscientious	logical
unique	active	clean
charismatic	empathetic	spiritually sound
sincere	reflective	independent
predictable	goal directed	receptive
assertive	dedicated	focused
exemplary	peaceful	consistent
understanding	cheerful	professional
achieving	knowledgeable	unstoppable
efficient	imaginative	objective
neat	realistic	graceful
congenial	fair minded	trusting
decisive	results oriented	authoritative
kind	productive	romantic

persistent	loving	prudent
adventurous	committed	warm
energetic	helpful	original
strong	intelligent	unbeatable
spontaneous	reliable	brave
determined	friendly	sensitive
likable	persuasive	ambitious
coachable	prominent	enthusiastic
cooperative	vigorous	teachable
insightful	orderly	distinctive
reassuring	supportive	masterful
forgiving	truthful	competent
happy	bold	introspective
proficient	self-confident	resourceful
vibrant	creative	fun loving
organized	agreeable	punctual
personable	entertaining	wise
trustworthy	talented	outgoing
beautiful	honest	unbreakable
self-aware	disciplined	caring
sexy	loyal	serious
affectionate	poised	articulate
enterprising	compassionate	steady
sympathetic	innovative	
courageous	remarkable	
direct	fun	

Choose to Write Down Compelling Goals

The very act of writing down and setting magnificent goals unlocks your creative powers, and the act of writing your goals is completely under your control.

In this lesson, you will learn to

- Motivate yourself to stick with goal setting
- Understand that real goals are written goals
- Learn a simple goal-setting process
- Develop clarity about your future
- Be able to share goals with someone you love
- Manage your goals effectively

Do you consider yourself an avid gambler? Most likely you do not, or you probably wouldn't be reading a book titled *Success Is Not an Accident.* But if at this moment you don't have specific measurable goals written down for each area of your life, and a plan for their accomplishment, then the odds are that success for you *will* be an accident. Cause and effect in your life will be unclear. Your future will be unpredictable, and your capacity to have an impact on the world with your unique talents and gifts will be severely diminished. You will passively accept a life by default rather than assertively choosing a life by design. This approach is not for you.

Intentional Living

As people have shared their success stories with me, I've found that every story has one thing in common: a goal. One of my favorite stories belongs to University of Georgia baseball coach David Perno, probably because it has to do with two of my favorite things: baseball and coaching. On July 21, 2001, two weeks after his thirty-fourth birthday, David became the youngest head baseball coach in the Southeast Conference.[1] But that's not the most impressive part of the story.

CHANGING FIELDS

Oddly enough, when you talk to David about his early goals, he doesn't mention baseball. Instead, he recalls his days playing football at Clarke Central High School in Athens, Georgia. It was David's football coach, Billy Henderson, who introduced him to goal setting. Henderson not only taught the boys on his team about winning—David's team won the state championship—he also talked to them about the importance of having a vision, dreaming big, and setting goals.

One of the first goals David set for himself was to play Division I football or baseball in college. It turned out that he would reach his goal by receiving an athletic scholarship to the University of Georgia, where as a freshman he would play left field for the school's baseball team. And in 1990, David would be a member of the team when they won the national championship.

A TURN OF EVENTS

Due to an injury in his first season, David could no longer play at his highest level. Surgery had slowed him down. So after the championship, David turned his sights to coaching.

During his senior year of college, David started writing down short-term goals. Two years later, as an assistant coach at Marshall University in West Virginia, David began focusing on what he wanted long-term.

"I knew what I wanted to do because I'd had the taste of it. I knew that I wanted to coach baseball, but I also knew I didn't want to stay in West Virginia too long. I wanted to return to the South. . . . I had to figure this thing out and plot my plan. And I laid it out on paper and put it in my wallet."[2]

REACHING THE GOAL

Getting married, having a child, and becoming the head baseball coach at the University of Georgia by age thirty-five—these were the three goals on David's list. "I knew the first thing I had to do was move back to Georgia, whether it was coaching high school, college, junior college, wherever. I had to get back in Georgia, make some contacts, and do a great job."[3]

David became an assistant coach to Robert Sapp at Middle Georgia Junior College. One year later he moved to the University of Georgia when Sapp was offered the job of head coach there. David stayed at the University of Georgia even after Sapp was replaced by Ron Polk, the winningest coach in Southeastern Conference history.[4] Under the direction of Polk and David, the Georgia team won the Southeastern Conference in 2001 and played in the College World Series.

At the end of the 2001 season, Polk returned to Mississippi State, where he had coached from 1976 to 1997.[5] This was the opportunity David had worked for. He had married Melaney Chastain in 1997, and their daughter was born in 1999, so with only one goal left on his original list, David threw away the piece of paper he had carried in his wallet for seven years. It was time to write down some new goals.

"I set this goal, and I had looked at this goal for many years. I evaluated it, and thirty-five was the cutoff. I was ready to walk away. I said, 'You know, it's going to work either way. If I don't get it now, then hey, I came up short. I've got to make some new goals and find a way to make them happen. If it does happen, you know it was meant to be.'"[6]

David got the job as head coach at the University of Georgia. But he does have some new goals. "Now I'm trying to get a little bit of balance, and I have spiritual, family, and health goals in addition to my career goals. And I think writing them down is the driving force. That's what gets me up every morning because there's so much to be done, so much to accomplish. And there's nothing better than checking off everything you've done at the end of the day."[7]

By writing down his goals, David set the course for his success. And he continues to write out new goals because he understands that success is not a onetime shot. After five seasons as head baseball coach of the University of Georgia, David has led the Bulldogs to the College World Series twice, attained a record of 183 wins and 126 losses, and has been honored as Baseball America's Coach of the Year.

What will your course look like? Will you get ready for extreme success or just hope to avoid failure?

This lesson will reinforce your need to set compelling goals, showing you how written goals and your mind are partners in your success. You will be motivated to do what is necessary to become the type of person you want to become. I'll explain why most Americans still don't set goals and show what you can do to avoid slipping into this trap of mediocrity. Understanding these concepts will prevent frustration and unnecessary trial and error. Next I'll give you the eight characteristics of effective goals and help you apply them to set yourself free from the limitations that hold you back. Then the foundation will be set, and you'll be ready to begin your goal-setting workshop, where I'll guide you step-by-step through the actual goal-setting process. Once you learn this process, you'll be able to adjust it, customize it, and mold it so that you can apply it to achieve every goal you desire. Finally, I'll introduce you to a simple system for managing your long- and short-range goals.

Remember, goal setting is the master skill of all lifelong success, yet it is practiced by less than 3 percent of the population. Only about one percent of people are fully goal directed, meaning that they have committed to doing only those things that help them accomplish a predetermined goal. Fortunately, goal setting and becoming goal directed are skills just like driving a car, skiing, cooking, operating a computer, and selling. And like those skills, there is no limit to how good you can become if you are willing to practice and are committed to becoming an expert.

When you become goal directed, this expertise spills over into all other compartments of your life, drawing out your full potential in each area. Goal setting is a critical skill. Even those who are genuinely proficient at setting goals can dramatically increase their productivity by upgrading, refining, and perfecting their goal-achieving skills. To stay sharp at any skill, you must keep an open mind to new ways of doing things. You must not become complacent. Keep in mind that there is nothing more dangerous to your future success than assuming that you're good at a critical skill when your knowledge is rudimentary at best. You must not think *good;* you must think *better.* If this sounds like your attitude, and you are serious about achieving greater personal and financial success, then the ideas in this lesson can help you progress further and faster than perhaps you ever thought possible.

Investing the time and brain power to set meaningful goals in each area of your life will produce internal, permanent motivation. You'll become inner directed rather than outer directed or other directed. You will experience an invigorating sense of control over your life. You'll be driven to become more competent with each passing day. Distractions will no longer be a challenge for you because your course is set.

Planning and reviewing your goals will provide you with an intense, laserlike focus. You will concentrate on the vital few instead of the trivial many. At every minute of every day, you will know exactly where you need to be and what you need to be doing. This enhanced effectiveness will excite you and generate the enthusiasm necessary to become a peak performer.

You will notice yourself getting up earlier and staying up later, and you'll still have boundless energy. As you concentrate more and more on your goals, you'll think less and less about your problems and worries. Your energies will be directed toward worthwhile tasks, and you'll refuse to participate in senseless, escapist activities that only deplete your energy, distract you from your goals, and delay your accomplishments. **Goals provide you with clarity of outcome, which is the prerequisite for becoming an outstanding decision maker.** When you know specifically where you are going, it's rather simple to assess opportunities and determine which ones are consistent with your objectives. Constantly remind yourself that every opportunity or activity is moving you either closer to the accomplishment of your goals or further away. The clock is always ticking. Nothing is neutral, and every single thing you do—or fail to do—counts!

While there are many important ingredients in the recipe of success, goals are most important. Without a doubt, the ability to set and achieve goals will do more to improve the quality of your life than any other single process you could ever learn. Whether we know it or not, we all have goals. The challenge is that the majority of the population has tiny goals with little if any motivational value. The masses tend to think small. Even those who have set high goals can get such a tremendous boost by mastering goal-setting principles that their lives will never again be the same. Most could-be superachievers choose to wing it. As a result, they fail to develop and multiply the potential they were born with.

Let's face it: We've all slacked off at some point. We have all settled for less than we could have had or accomplished. So now, this minute, let's create a turning point! Together let's commit to raising our standards. Remember, everything counts!

The Importance of Goal Setting

Learning to set goals and crafting plans for their accomplishment will have more of a positive impact on your life than anything else you could possibly do. As the saying goes, "If you don't know where you are going, any road will take you there." Goals serve as points on a road map, detailing how to achieve success in a logical sequence. While this sounds

Here's the Proof

At the beginning of an address to an audience of 150 employees at their annual company retreat, I asked everyone to stand up. Then I asked everyone who did not have goals to sit down. A handful of people sat. I then asked everyone who did not have written goals to sit down. Unfortunately, but not surprisingly, all but about twenty people sat. Next, I asked those remaining to sit down unless they had written goals for more than just their career or financial life. That eliminated another twelve, leaving only eight of 150 people who had written goals targeting more than finances or career. I asked the remaining eight to sit down unless they had a written plan that accompanied their goals. That question filtered out five more, leaving three of 150 who had written goals and a plan in more than just the financial area. I asked the remaining three (all senior management, including the company president) to sit down unless they reviewed their goals on a daily basis. Only one person remained standing (a vice president of sales).

Only one in 150 had written goals in more areas than just financial, had a plan for accomplishing them, and reviewed the goals daily. This is consistently what I've found over the years as I've surveyed the attendees in my public events. Invariably, less than 3 percent have written goals, and even those who have written down their goals have often done so only regarding finances or career.

You may have heard of the 1953 study of Yale graduates. The subjects were periodically interviewed and followed by researchers for more than twenty years. Eventually the graduates were again interviewed, tested, and surveyed. Results showed that 3 percent of the Yale graduates earned more money than all of the other 97 percent put together! The only difference between them was that the top 3 percent had written goals and a plan of action for those goals, which they reviewed daily.

Harvard University later did a study of business-school graduates from the class of 1979. They found that, other than to "enjoy themselves," 84 percent of the class had no goals at all. Thirteen percent had goals and plans but had not written them down. Only 3 percent of the Harvard class had written goals accompanied by a plan of action. In 1989, the class was resurveyed. The results showed that the 13 percent who at least had mental goals were earning twice as much as the 84 percent with no goals. However, the 3 percent who had written down their goals and drafted a plan of action were earning ten times as much as the other 97 percent combined!

The point is clear: Having written goals will make you more successful, and having written, well-planned goals that you review daily will make you super successful.

so obvious, the unfortunate truth is that most people take it for granted. They have only a vague idea of where point A is, and no clue at all about point B. Most people spend more time planning their summer vacations and their weddings than they do planning their lives and their marriages. Most people major in minor things. They get caught up in the things that keep them busy but contribute very little to the overall quality of their lives. Keep in mind that big goals generate lots of motivation and energy, while small goals

What is the most magnificent goal you can pursue in the next three years?

produce little motivation. Pursuing your goals should be fun and interesting, like a cherished hobby. In other words, you need to design goals that really inspire you—that are so interesting, motivating, and stimulating that you'll get up by 5 a.m. and stay up burning the midnight oil.

Intelligence, education, hard work, and good connections are useful, but without goals, you tend to drift like a rudderless ship from project to project, never harnessing your full potential. Without goals, you can get by and even do well according to society's standards, but you will never come close to realizing your unique gifts. Without goals, you will likely compare and measure yourself against others rather than against your own God-given potential.

Many have called goal setting the master skill of success because it is the essential ingredient for successful living. Without it, you can never come close to living your life to its fullest. With it, you can learn and master anything else you desire. But you can't become an expert at setting goals through just one exposure to a CD or by attending a seminar. Mastery doesn't come without deliberate, repetitive practice and a constant desire for never-ending advancement and improvement.

The primary benefit of mastering the skill of goal setting is that **you begin to take personal control of your life.** The overwhelming majority of Americans are so caught up in the urgent activities of daily living that they seem to be sprinting in a dense fog. They are running hard but going nowhere. **They've confused** *activity* **with** *accomplishment.*

Without goals, one does not live; one simply exists, drifting. Your

Top 10 Reasons to Establish Written Goals for Your Life

10 | Written goals strengthen your character by promoting a long-term perspective.

9 | Written goals allow you to lead your life as opposed to simply managing it.

8 | Written goals provide internal, permanent, and consistent motivation.

7 | Written goals help you stay focused—to concentrate on what's most important.

6 | Written goals enhance your decision-making ability.

5 | Written goals simultaneously require and build self-confidence.

4 | Written goals help you create the future in advance.

3 | Written goals help you to control changes—to adjust your sails, to work with the wind rather than against it.

2 | Written goals heighten your awareness of opportunities that are consistent with your goals.

1 | And finally, the most important benefit of setting effective goals is the **person you become** as a result of the pursuit!

life and your future will be determined by what comes along and attracts your attention. Denis Waitley writes, "The reason most people don't reach their goals is that they don't define them, learn about them, or ever seriously consider them as believable or achievable. Winners can tell you where they are going, what they plan to do along the way, and who will be sharing the adventure with them."[8]

Those without clearly defined goals are continually tempted by every fashionable trend society serves up. Mediocrity is best defined as failing to set big goals for your life and neglecting to live the life God gave you. If we don't routinely set challenging goals, we can become satisfied with surprisingly little. It's easy to descend gradually into complacency and start accepting less than the best for yourself and your family. **Mediocrity breeds mediocrity.** If you don't have a definite purpose, you'll invariably drift in whichever direction the wind happens to be blowing. Instead of being assertive and proactive with your life, you'll simply react to the world around you and become, as most do, the self-induced victim of circumstances.

On the other hand, with definite goals, you psychologically shield yourself from being influenced by fads and other popular distractions. You may notice these crazes and trends and even listen to some of them, but the existence of your definite, written goals will quickly steer you back to your predetermined path.

People who experience long-term, consistent success avoid reaching into too many baskets. They deliberately concentrate on a single purpose that permits them to be their absolute best. With goals, you'll experience daily contentment because each day you will move closer to the things most important to you. You'll be able to chart your progress and be inspired by what you've already done. As a result, you'll gain momentum, and your successes will begin to snowball as your confidence grows and your ambitions expand. People without written goals don't have a sense of where they are. Like driving on an unmarked highway on a cloudy day, they don't know if they're going north, south, east, or west. They have few mechanisms for constructive feedback and accountability. By contrast, the positive pressure created by setting clearly defined goals activates your inborn creativity and allows your unique talents to rise to the surface.

You were created and blessed with unlimited potential and the ability to make your life a masterpiece. **The least you can do is set challenging, specific goals that will force you to stretch and increase your contribution to the lives of others.**

Adopt an extended, long-term perspective. You excel in life to the extent that you apply a long-term perspective in making your most important decisions.

I hope I've sold or re-sold you on the importance of goals and the impact they can have on you, your family, your career, and your future. I want you not only to know about goals but to live goals! You can function at your best as a human being only when you are actively pursuing a set of meaningful goals.

Psychological Blocks to Goal Setting

With all these benefits, why don't more people set goals? What are the psychological blocks that trick most people into just winging it through life? The next few pages will explain these blocks and show you why many people fail so that you can be alert to these tendencies in yourself and others. I will explain the human characteristics that lead to underachievement, frustration, and mediocrity so you can consciously try to counteract them. If your objective is to develop and maximize your virtues, or your successful qualities, it's very important that you also understand your vices, or the areas that may hold you back.

WHY PEOPLE DON'T SET GOALS

The number one reason people don't set goals is that they have not yet accepted personal responsibility for their lives. Albert Schweitzer said, "Man must cease attributing his problems to his environment and learn again to exercise his will—his personal responsibility." The starting point of all personal success is the acceptance of 100 percent responsibility for your life. Until you have claimed total and unconditional responsibility for everything that happens in your life, you'll never be serious about goal setting. Irresponsible people are like a leaf blowing in the wind with zero hope of steering itself in a meaningful direction. "*Qué será, será!* Whatever will be, will be." is their constant refrain. They reason that because some events are out of their control (such as stock-market fluctuations, the weather, or the death of loved ones), all things must be out of their control. If things are out of their control, then why should they even bother trying to control them? After all, it's a whole lot easier to put the blame for a mediocre life on someone else's shoulders. Remember this point: As Emerson put it, "No one can cheat you out of ultimate success but yourself." We have all been blessed with freedom of choice, and we will go nowhere until and unless we accept unqualified responsibility for our lives. We covered this in lesson 1. Keep in mind that prizes do not go to those who have been treated fairly but to those who have maturely accepted responsibility.

Another reason people don't set goals is *fear of criticism,* which often develops during childhood. Parents, teachers, and other adults often discourage us inadvertently by pointing out all the reasons why we can't achieve a particular goal. Their intentions are usually good. They don't want us to get our hopes up and then be disappointed. But the end result is that we stop creating compelling goals and dreams for our futures because we don't want to experience the pain of having them squashed. Each time an authority figure reacts negatively to a child's expressed desire, the child becomes increasingly more hesitant to express those desires or goals. By the time we become adults, the hesitancy to desire something has become a reluctance to set goals, or at least goals that are out of the ordinary. (And those are the most fun!) **It is difficult to become goal directed in a world that is centered on limitations.** Our peers often laugh at us when we talk about doing or becoming something they can't imagine for themselves. They may belittle your desire to start your own business, get into a career you truly love, become wealthy, or really commit to growing in your faith. Since nobody likes to be ridiculed, we learn to

> **Obstacles are the raw materials of great accomplishments.**

Seven Reasons People Don't Set Goals

1 | They have not yet accepted personal responsibility for their lives.

2 | They fear criticism.

3 | They don't know how.

4 | They don't realize the importance of goals.

5 | They experienced the curse of early success.

6 | They fear failure.

7 | They fear success.

shut up and keep our dreams to ourselves, eventually forgetting what we wanted or even why we embraced those dreams. We learn to play it safe, to go along, and to not rock the boat. Unfortunately, this attitude of conformity and underachievement is transported into adulthood, where we continue to sell ourselves short.

A third reason why people do not set goals is that they simply *don't know how*. Even if you earn an advanced degree in our society, you've probably never had any formal instruction on how to set, manage, and achieve personal goals. Virtually none of my MBA clients have ever had a single course on goal setting. This is a serious void because goal setting is the master subject, the skill that makes all other subjects useful and practical. Herbert Spencer writes, "The great aim of education is not knowledge, but action." At least it should be. Remember that to know but not act is to truly not know. To think you know something but not really know it is a prescription for underachievement.

I've invested countless hours researching the concept of goal setting. I've devoted most of my adult life to teaching individuals, couples, kids, and organizations how to set goals effectively. Even so, I learn something or make a new distinction about goals nearly every day. That's why it still amazes me to have others claim they know it all already.

A fourth reason people don't set goals is that they *don't realize the importance of goals.* If you grew up in a home where goal setting and success were not topics of conversation around the dinner table, then simple ignorance may be holding you back. If your network of friends and acquaintances do not have clearly written goals, then it will be natural for you to ignore yours as well. Be careful who you spend your time with, for you will inevitably start to think and act just like them.

A fifth reason people don't set goals is what I call *the curse of early success.* Many individuals experience success early in their lives, then become smug and stop growing and improving. They may do well in college, get a prominent first job, or maybe even receive a rapid promotion. Their early success gives them a false sense of security. Those who fall prey to this curse are often pointed in the right direction but never do anything other than coast. This is a route of compromise. Do you know people who are making a decent living or earning good money but not doing a whole lot more with their lives? When asked about their goals, these people give you a surprised stare and then reply that they're "on the right track." "Settle, settle, settle" is their theme song.

A sixth reason people fail to set goals—and perhaps the most common—is *fear of failure.* Many people are afraid to set goals because they fear that by setting a goal, they and others will be able to determine whether or not they have succeeded. This is an especially important point because those who fear failure are other- and outer-directed individuals. They are afraid of what others may think of them, and they are afraid of what they may think of themselves. Winners follow their inner voice rather than the outer voices of the masses. People who suffer from the fear of failure harbor the subconscious thought, *If I don't try, I can't fail.* Of course, this is nonsense—a convenient cop-out. Winners know that the only true failure is failing to try. **Failing to set written goals is the precise equivalent of not trying.**

Parents may promote fear of failure in their children by making their love and praise conditional on specific accomplishments. When a child believes that a parent's love depends on achievements, he or she often becomes paralyzed with fear and unable to set challenging

> When you choose to write down compelling goals, you are simultaneously choosing a compelling future. Exciting goals foreshadow an exciting future.

goals. The child finds more comfort in not trying than in risking failure. Conversely, the child who experiences unconditional love is likely to be assertive, ambitious, emotionally healthy, and eager to express himself or herself through a variety of pursuits.

Keep in mind that fear, while common, is a totally unnatural and unnecessary state of mind. The Bible says, "God has not given us a spirit of fear, but of power and of love and of a sound mind" (2 Timothy 1:7, NKJV). Psychologists say that newborns have two fears: the fear of loud noises and the fear of falling. For the most part, though, we grow out of these fears. Later we learn a series of other fears that are, for the most part, irrational. These fears are unproductive and inconsistent with the abundant and joy-filled life we were created to experience.

And finally, a seventh reason people don't set goals is *fear of success.* This may sound strange, but nonetheless it's a predominant reason why many people fail to set goals. They are raised with the belief that it is somehow wrong or sinful to pursue our desires or to exceed average performance. Therefore, many people strive to be just like everyone else, sometimes even appearing to apologize for their accomplishments. They fear standing out or being different for any reason, even if it means sacrificing their success. Wouldn't it make more sense to emulate the peak performers rather than the underachievers? Don't we have enough of the average already? **The Bible is clear that God loves excellence.** The apostle Paul writes, "Whatever you do, work at it with all your heart, as working for the Lord, not for men" (Colossians 3:23, NIV). In Ecclesiastes 9:10, Solomon writes, "Whatever your hand finds to do, do it with all your might" (NIV).

A variation of the fear of success is the fear of failure at the next level. Some people are afraid that if they succeed, they will feel pressure to repeat their success. To avoid having to live up to this new standard, they procrastinate and never give it their best, hoping that their lack of competence and confidence at the current level will remain a secret. This type of fear often manifests itself as subconscious, self-sabotaging behavior and is just as common in the business world as in personal relationships.

Eight Rules for Highly Effective Goals

When you follow each of the following eight rules, you can expect to develop your full potential and join the top one percent of high achieving men and women. Many skeptics and underachievers have haphazardly attempted goal setting without following these rules and failed as a result—erroneously concluding that goal setting does not work, at least not for them. Goals work for anyone who is subject to the law of gravity—that is, everyone. To ensure your success, follow these simple guidelines faithfully, and the results will speak for themselves.

1. HIGHLY EFFECTIVE GOALS ARE WRITTEN!

Putting things in writing is by far the most important step in goal setting. Wishes and fantasies are transformed into goals through the act of writing them down. By putting your goals on paper, you make them concrete, tangible, and physically real. Many studies have shown that people who write down their goals are ten times more likely to achieve them than those who have only mental goals. Similar research shows that people with written goals earn ten to one hundred times more than equally gifted individuals who neglect to put their goals in writing. **Writing down your goals helps you to crystallize your thinking and gives you a physical device for focusing your attention.** It stimulates your brain's reticular activating system, which is the mechanism within your brain that controls your awareness. When you are more conscious of your goals, you will notice the people, resources, information, and opportunities that will help you achieve them.

Written goals also create a scorecard that you can later evaluate and learn from. They help you measure your success and progress in life. Having your goals on paper also increases your self-confidence. Being able to see that you accomplished something you decided in advance will give you a powerful

Not knowing how you are going to accomplish a goal is never a valid excuse for not setting the goal. First write the goal down. Then work to figure out how to reach it.

sense of self-worth and will encourage you to set more challenging goals in the future. Your successes will begin to snowball! Writing goals on paper forms an accountability contract with yourself, which automatically strengthens your character and boosts your self-confidence. Remember, in our society we assign a higher value to written agreements than oral agreements. They simply hold up better. So make your goals written contracts with yourself! When people tell me they don't need to write their goals down because they have them in their mind, I know they are really copping out and eventually will miss out.

2. HIGHLY EFFECTIVE GOALS ARE STATED IN PRESENT TENSE.

I encourage you to state each goal as if its accomplishment were already a fact. For example, "I earn $125,000 this year" or "I lower my golf handicap to 10 by June 25." Writing goals like this allows you to recruit your mind to help you reach your goals. An obvious discrepancy between where you'd like to be and where you are currently creates what is called structural tension or dissonance in your mind. There's a gap between reality and your vision for the future, and since your mind hates tension of any kind, it immediately begins to alert you to all sorts of people, resources, and breakthroughs that can help push you toward a goal. In essence, *your mind creates a new field of sight.* Stating a goal in the present tense communicates that goal to your brain in the most effective format, allowing you to visualize the goal clearly and to believe that it is possible. It signifies to your conscious and subconscious mind that you are not where you want to be.

Refuse to state your goal as "I will do this" or "I will accomplish that." When you use the phrase *I will*, you mentally push your achievement some-where off into the vague, distant future. There is less pressure to come up with strategies to achieve your goal and to take immediate action. Using "I will" promotes procrastination, and of course we want to put that off as long as possible!

> If you don't have specific goals written down for your life, you are mentally mal-nourished. Your mind was designed to be fed with goals just as your body was de-signed to be fed with food and water.

3. HIGHLY EFFECTIVE GOALS ARE STATED POSITIVELY.

One example of a positive goal is "I eat healthy, nutritious foods" instead of "I no longer eat junk food." It's important to avoid stating, writing, or talking about your goals in a negative way. Why? Because we think in pictures. Words are simply symbols for thoughts and ideas. Every time you write or say a word, you evoke a vision in your mind. And you can't evoke a vision of not doing something. You may say, "I don't eat junk food," but your subconscious mind only processes, "I eat junk food." It simply omits the "not" and shows you the "I eat junk food" vision. If you say, "I am not fat," your brain simply sees, understands, and goes to work on "I am fat." If you say, "I am not hitting the ball into the water," all your mind goes to work on is, "I am hitting the ball into the water." (Now that you know this, you can wreak havoc with your golf friends by reminding them of the water just as they are about to take their shot. And they'll usually respond, "I'm not going to hit it into the water." But the reverse is often exactly what they do!) **Remember, you will always act consistently with the dominant pictures you allow to occupy your mind.** You must state your goal in a positive way so that your mind will understand it accurately and go to work on it. The reason most people state goals in negative terms is that they are much more aware of what they *don't* want than what they *do* want. But whatever you're most aware of is what you experience. If you're aware of nice people, you'll start to bump into more nice people. If you're aware of your goals, you'll reach more of your goals. If you're conscious of ways to serve others, you'll find those opportunities. And along the way, a lot of people will call you lucky.

4. HIGHLY EFFECTIVE GOALS ARE CONSISTENT WITH YOUR PERSONAL MISSION STATEMENT.

Your goals should cause you to grow more like the person you were created to become. They should be personally meaningful to you. Many people make the mistake of setting goals that are meaningful to someone else or that will please someone else but that evoke no passion in their own lives. The best way to keep your commitment to reach a goal is to understand why you are striving for it. It's the *why*, or the link to your values, that keeps you motivated.

Effective goals are best established after you thoroughly think through your values and compose your personal mission statement. Values are those things that are most important to you. They include people, things, virtues, concepts, beliefs, and feelings. Together they constitute your individ-

> When you establish and wholeheartedly pursue goals that are consistent with your highest values, you grow more like the person you were created to become, thereby satisfying and fulfilling your purpose.

ual philosophy of life, or your personal vision. Goals are intended to help you experience your unique purpose in life. Trouble arises when we set goals without first clarifying what we stand for and who we want to become as human beings. We often accept and adopt others' values because we've never invested the mental effort to determine what's truly important to us. When we set goals that are not in harmony with our personal values, we may still end up being high achievers, but the achievement will be accompanied by a feeling of emptiness, a feeling of "Is this it? Is this all there is?" Most unhappiness and negative stress come from proclaiming internally that something or someone is most important to us but then acting based on different priorities. Consider these questions:

Am I designing my life around principle-based values?

Who am I becoming by pursuing this goal?

Will accomplishing this goal add to my peace of mind?

Make sure that each of your goals is connected to a particular value or role in life. There should be a deep and obvious connection between your goals and your personal mission statement. In fact, pursuing your goals should force you to become more like the person described in your personal mission statement. For example, if part of your mission statement emphasizes investing quantity time with your children, avoid setting a community service goal that will likely require you to spend many evenings away from home. That will contradict your value of family time. In another season of life, community service may be a completely appropriate goal.

5. HIGHLY EFFECTIVE GOALS ARE SPECIFIC AND MEASURABLE.

There must be no fuzziness or ambiguity whatsoever in your stated goals. Each goal must be measurable so that you or someone else can evaluate your progress objectively and determine exactly when you have achieved the goal—or if a new course of action should be taken. The more specific your goal is, the more clear you will be about what steps you must take to achieve it, and the more focused you will be. **The more you are focused on your goal, the more you'll be aware of the people, ideas, and resources around you that can help you reach your goal.** A clear direction also tends to increase your motivation and enthusiasm. It spurs you to take action.

Often in my coaching sessions clients ask, "How specific do my goals need to be?" I always answer, "Can you be more specific?" If it is possible to be more specific, then you should be. Keep asking yourself: "How can

Highly Effective Goals Are

- Written

- Stated in the present tense

- Stated positively

- Time bound

- Challenging and reasonable

- Specific and measurable

- Consistent with your personal
  mission statement

- Thoroughly planned

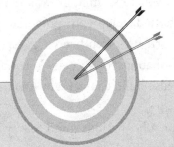

I define this goal more clearly? How can I make it more precise?" Goals like "I want to be happy," "I want to have a better marriage," or "I want to earn lots of money and be rich" don't cut it. They offer no unambiguous goal to shoot for. Nothing is measurable. There is little or no purpose, and nothing much gets done. Vague and hazy objectives produce diluted results! You'll find that your creativity will increase as you more clearly define your goal. Creativity demands pressure. Being concrete and very specific provides this pressure.

6. HIGHLY EFFECTIVE GOALS ARE TIME BOUND.

Deadlines put positive pressure on you to take action. Without concrete deadlines, it's just human nature to keep putting things off. Strangely enough, we tend to procrastinate on goals that are most valuable to our long-term peace of mind. We keep postponing those actions that can really increase the quality of our lives! We often get stuck in a rut, in the deadly confines of the comfort zone. **Comfort is often confused with success, and complacency is the result.** To avoid this complacency, make sure your goals are time bound with reasonable deadlines for accomplishment. It's very important that the time you allow is reasonable! It's been said that there is no such thing as an unrealistic goal, just an unrealistic time frame in which to accomplish it. Learn from each experience you have with goal setting so that you become progressively more accurate at determining deadlines.

7. HIGHLY EFFECTIVE GOALS ARE REASONABLE AND CHALLENGING.

Goals should cause you to stretch, grow, and get out of your comfort zone. In order to fully develop your potential, you must be willing to experience discomfort. It's often been suggested that people set goals with a fifty-fifty probability of success. You want to set goals that are achievable but that also build character by exercising your self-discipline and perseverance.

In order for your subconscious mind to buy into your goal, the goal must have some degree of believability. For example, imagine you're driving a fifteen-year-old Chevy, but you've always had this thing for a Rolls-

Royce. Think about stopping at a traffic light in your Chevy and having a Rolls pull up alongside you. Would seeing that Rolls motivate you to take action—to drive straight to a Rolls-Royce dealer? Would it cause you to want to really stretch yourself? Would it be a powerful inspiration? Most likely it would not.

The reason? The gap between where you are now—driving the old Chevy—and where you

 Your talent, skill, and creativity will rise to meet the level of goal you set for yourself. So think huge!

want to go—driving a Rolls-Royce—is simply beyond believability. Your mind just wouldn't accept the idea that you could own a Rolls-Royce, because it has no consistent prior experiences or beliefs on which to base such an idea. That doesn't mean there's no hope for you. Rather, it means that you need to set some intermediate goals that will act as stepping-stones to gradually raise your beliefs and self-concept to that of someone driving a Rolls. For instance, you could first set a goal for driving a low-end luxury car, and then set another goal for driving a top-of-the-line Mercedes. Ultimately, you could drive whatever type of car you desired.

Here's a nonmonetary example of the same idea. Imagine you've been thirty pounds overweight for most of your adult life. Even though you've worked really hard to lose the excess fat, and you've had a goal to get back to your high school weight, it just hasn't happened yet. Think about being in your car at a traffic light when an extremely fit jogger passes by. Would seeing that obviously lean and fit athlete motivate you to increase your exercise routine and drastically improve your diet? Would it cause you to want to stretch yourself? Would it be a powerful inspiration? Most likely it would not, for the same reason seeing a Rolls-Royce doesn't motivate the Chevy owner. The gap between where you are now (overweight and out of shape) and where you want to go (becoming lean, strong, and fit) is simply beyond believability. Your mind just would not accept the idea that you could be trim and healthy, because it has no recent or consistent prior experiences or beliefs. This does not mean there's no hope for you. Rather, it means that you need to set some intermediate goals that will act as stepping stones to gradually raise your beliefs and self-concept to that of someone who is in great physical condition. For instance, you could first set a goal to drop one belt notch or dress size, and then set another goal to lose ten pounds. Ultimately, you could be as lean and healthy as you desired.

The point is to get your mind working with you, not against you. The way to accomplish this is to **set goals that push the envelope, that are just slightly outside what you currently believe about yourself.** Goals like these activate your natural creativity, supplying you with insights for achievement that otherwise would not have occurred to you. By contrast, goals that are unreasonable (at least at this point in your development) lock up your creativity and tend to act as de-motivators. As you become more of an expert at goal setting, as your confidence grows, you'll see how simple it is to incrementally strengthen your belief in yourself by setting and then achieving progressively more-challenging goals. You may set goals that have only a 20 or 30 percent chance of success, but that's better than setting your goals too low. If you're going to make a mistake, err on the side of aiming too high.

8. HIGHLY EFFECTIVE GOALS ARE THOROUGHLY PLANNED.

You should have tangible action steps for each of your goals. You need to compile the details, make a plan, write out all the activities, prioritize them, organize them, and rewrite them as often as necessary to make your plan perfect. Revise it, improve it, plan, and think on paper. It's also a good idea to consider developing several backup plans, just as a good general would do. Exercise your mind by anticipating various contingencies and deciding how you would respond swiftly and effectively. All great leaders train themselves to be great planners. For smaller goals, developing a plan will be a quick exercise. For huge goals, the planning process may require several hours or even several days.

The Goal-Setting Workshop

I'm going to share with you a powerful, practical, and effective goal formula. If you will follow this method, and if you will exercise the self-discipline to put it into practice on a regular basis, your results will be phenomenal.

STEP #1: BRAINSTORM YOUR DREAMS

Take out a pad of paper and a pen or pencil—or, if you prefer, sit down at your computer or pull out your PDA. Find a quiet place where you will not be disturbed for at least thirty minutes. At the top of a blank sheet of paper write "The Next Thirty Years." Now begin to brainstorm about anything and everything you have ever wanted to be, do, or have. This is often called unlimited wishing or dreaming, and it's the first tangible step in becoming goal directed.

Creating this list requires no resources other than a small amount of time, some mental effort, and a few sheets of paper. And it will provide the foundation for a more successful, exciting, and fulfilling life. It stimulates your creativity and will help you notice opportunities. As you're brainstorming, it's important not to impose any limitations—real or imagined—such as money, age, sex, race, family, children, education, connections, or anything else. Be careful of letting limits turn into excuses that eventually spoil your opportunities for getting more out of life. As we learned in lesson 1, no matter how big your favorite excuse is, somebody somewhere has had it far worse and still succeeded in spite of all perceived disadvantages. Limits have power over you and your future only to the degree that you let them.

Suspend all judgment on whether you can achieve what you want or whether you are worthy of it. *Just write it down!*

There is no limit, other than the power of your imagination, to the number of desires you can include on your personal wish list. The key to this exercise is to write down everything you can imagine without letting your mind stop. Think of your wish list as a grand script for the movie of your life! You are, after all, the writer, producer, director, and star. You can take your movie in any direction you choose, and you can fill the script with as much passion, adventure, joy, and positive experiences as you can imagine or desire. Remember that what you write down is your preview of life's coming attractions.

You will find that merely completing this simple brainstorming process will produce a renewed sense of enthusiasm for your future. You will experience an inner excitement, a surge of vitality, and positive anticipation.

Once you've written down everything you could ever possibly want, look over your list and make sure you have some challenging financial goals. Make sure you have goals for your marriage and other key relationships. How about goals as a parent? Do you have fitness goals? Are there any new health habits you could develop? What about your personal growth? What new things do you want to learn? How many books do you want to read next year? Did you write down any spiritual goals? This time next year, where do you want to be in your faith? If you want to make it happen, you'd better write it down.

Think about the many areas of your life: faith, family, health, energy, relationships, career, finances, and personal development. Make sure you have goals for each area where you want to experience growth. To lead a fully satisfying life, you need a balance of goals. So, whatever it is, write it down.

Once you've written down your goals, take time to consider them carefully in prayer. Ask God to give you wisdom about which goals to pursue. He may bring ideas to your mind that aren't already on your list, or he may show you that some of your dreams are not in line with his best for you. As people of faith, we should seek God's blessing and approval. After all, "Unless the LORD builds the house, its builders labor in vain" (Psalm 127:1, NIV).

Write it down, and then make it happen!

At least once a year, revise and review your list. Many of my 1% Club clients have found this exercise so refreshing and stimulating that they practice it two or three times a year. Try it for yourself and see.

STEP #2: CREATE YOUR IDEAL LIFESTYLE

Proper planning requires that you look into the distant future and create a vivid mental image of the life you'd like to be leading. This will become your personal vision for the future. The number of years you project can

Questions to Help You
Start Your Brainstorm Session

———————— *Remember, no limits!* ————————

- What do you want to have?
- What do you want to be?
- Who do you want to become?
- What extraordinary things would you like to do?
- What kind of impact do you want to have on your profession?
- If you were absolutely unafraid, what would you try to do?
- How could you turn one of your hobbies into a business?
- Where do you want to go? Who do you want to go with?
- What would you like the quality of your marriage to be?
- Spiritually, are you headed in the right direction?
- What do you want to share with others?
- What charities do you want to support?
- How much money do you want to donate in your lifetime?
- How could you better exploit your Genius to serve and benefit others?
- Would you like to skydive or scuba dive? What other activities would you like to try?
- Would you like to have a personal trainer? How about a personal success coach?
- What experiences do you want to have with your children before they go to college? after college?
- Are there any famous people you would like to meet? Who?
- Would you like to become famous? By excelling at what?
- How much passion do you want to have in your marriage?
- Would you like to become a millionaire? How about a billionaire?
- Do you want to work for someone else the rest of your life?

More Brainstorming Questions

- What would you like your net worth to be when you retire? At what age would you like to retire?
- What new things would you like to learn?
- How involved could you be with your children and grandchildren?
- Would you like to conquer the fear of public speaking?
- What character traits would you like to develop?
- What silly things would you like to do?
- If you had unlimited time, talent, finances, knowledge, self-confidence, and support from your family, how would your life change?
- What would you like to witness taking place in your lifetime?
- What one great thing would you dare to attempt if you absolutely knew you could not fail?

vary depending on your experience with goals and your current comfort level. Some of my clients go as far out as thirty years; others go nine to twenty-one. The point is to be as clear as possible about the vital details of the life and lifestyle you'd like to enjoy in the future. The reason for looking so far ahead is that, eventually, you're going to end up there. To make sure your actions and choices today match up with the life you want tomorrow, you must begin with the end result in mind. You have to know where you're headed. **You cannot live effectively if you have only short-term goals.** It takes a long-term vision and long-range goals to reveal the most appropriate short-term goals. So look at your life as an integrated whole. Approach life with the big picture in mind, and mentally project yourself into the future. Try for at least nine years.

Using the ideas generated from your brainstorm in step one, write

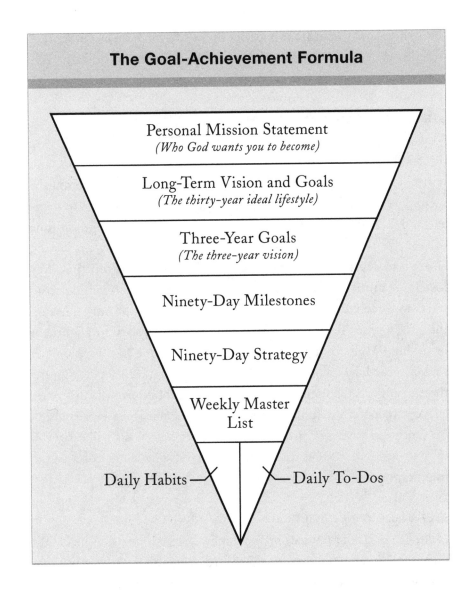

The Goal-Achievement Formula

Personal Mission Statement
(Who God wants you to become)

Long-Term Vision and Goals
(The thirty-year ideal lifestyle)

Three-Year Goals
(The three-year vision)

Ninety-Day Milestones

Ninety-Day Strategy

Weekly Master List

Daily Habits ———X   X——— Daily To-Dos

a two- or three-paragraph description of your ideal lifestyle. A bullet-point list is fine, too. Write in the present tense, as if what you're describing were already true.

Be sure to include details about your health, marriage, faith, major accomplishments, things you're grateful for, hobbies, energy level, net worth, amount of free time, peace of mind, and anything else you can think of. Now make a note of the most obvious milestones you need to see along the way in order to experience the life you have just described. You can view these benchmarks as the subgoals that need to be met before your long-term vision can become a reality.

STEP #3: TAKE THE THREE-YEAR LEAP

Now that you have some ideas about your future, let's tackle the midterm by creating clear, specific, measurable, achievable, and, most important, written three-year goals and their corresponding plans for accomplishment. I've found that three years is the perfect amount of time to manage and do really big things with your life. It's the ideal length of time to visualize your life being significantly different. **Three years is long enough to achieve some gigantic goals but not so far out that they lose their motivational pull.** Your three-year goals, stretching from today to three years out, are intended to be subgoals or milestones on the way to your long-term vision. Make sure they are in alignment by asking, "Will accomplishing these goals lead me to my vision?" If so, how exactly? Double-check yourself by asking, "Does pursuing my three-year goals represent the best route to my long-term vision?" After all, your vision of the future should determine your three-year goals.

Once you have established that your three-year goals will carry you to your vision, it's time to convince yourself why these goals are so important.

STEP #4: CONVINCE YOURSELF

Next, list all of the rewards of accomplishing your goals. What's in it for you? Why do you want to achieve these goals? Keep in mind that the more and better reasons you have, the more motivated you will be. Each goal will present tangible rewards and intangible benefits. Think about the emotions you'll enjoy as a result of achieving each goal, and think about the material rewards you'll receive. Write them down. Exaggerate a little bit. The more powerful you can make this purpose—your "why"—the better. Make sure you have enough reasons for accomplishing your goals; if you have enough, you can accomplish anything. Keep in mind that reasons precede answers. First determine the what. Next figure out the why, and then the how! When you know what you want and when you want it, you can always find a way to make it happen.

STEP #5: PLAN ON PAPER

Planning is the hallmark of the mature, responsible, and self-reliant human being. In fact, almost every failure can be traced back to lack of proper planning.

Planning is the deliberate act of pulling the future into the present so you can do something about the future right now. **You must change your habits and other behaviors** *now* **to reap rewards in the fu-**

> Great leaders possess tremendous long-term clarity about what they're trying to accomplish both personally and in their careers. And it's this long-term perspective that builds character, wisdom, and self-discipline. Long-term thinking is the hallmark of high-performance living, yet it's often neglected in favor of the treadmill of urgent activities of the moment.

ture. If you want your future to be different, you must make things different in the present. **Things don't improve by themselves!** You must do something different to bring about the new results you are seeking.

Many people don't understand what planning is. They interpret the word *planning* as simply transferring into their calendar miscellaneous appointments and to-dos from the backside of envelopes, cocktail napkins, and Post-it notes without any regard to long-term goals or a personal mission.

Planning really means evaluating your life in light of where you've been, where you are now, and where you intend to go. **You must be willing to question how well you've managed your life until now.** Effective planning allows you to avoid life management by crisis. Crises divert your attention from the vital people and activities in your life and are nearly always a result of inadequate planning. Systematic, long-term, yearly, quarterly, monthly, weekly, and daily planning is absolutely critical to your success. Remind yourself that all successful people plan on paper. Unsuccessful people simply "can't seem to find the time."

Be aware that plans are rarely 100 percent accurate. However, you must not fall into the trap of thinking, "Well, since I cannot have a perfect plan . . . since I cannot eliminate all interruptions . . . since I cannot eliminate all urgencies . . . why bother to eliminate any of them?" That's crooked logic and a cop-out for failing to try. Let go of any tendencies you have toward misplaced perfectionism and focus instead on the strategic planning that will take your life to a higher level. Invest considerable time in your plan. Keep in mind that you will be rewriting, revising, and improving your plan as you progress toward your goals.

The starting point of three-year planning is to envision yourself already in possession of your three-year goals and then work back to the present. This means that you must mentally project yourself into the future to the time and place where each goal will be a reality. From this vantage point, look back to the present and critically assess the steps you must take to reach the goal. This "back from the future" exercise sharpens your perception and solidifies your strategy. It develops the habit of outcome-based thinking, or results orientation. This is helpful for your short-term goals as well as your major lifetime goals. Constantly feed your mind a vivid picture of the end result you're striving for. Then develop your plan by working from the accomplishment of a goal back to the present.

Your three-year goals should be, in essence, action steps or subgoals leading up to your long-term vision. It's easy to talk about what we want, but the hard part is putting plans on paper, where they actually mean something.

So from the perspective of having accomplished your three-year goals, begin to work your way back to today. Consider what must be accomplished by the end of year two and then by the end of year one. At this point, the end of year one, you have a set of one-year goals. To translate this into action, think about what you need to accomplish in the fourth quarter. What do you need to accomplish by the third quarter? the second quarter? And finally, in the first quarter? This is the basic concept of strategic planning. As you can see, we're counting backward in time from a midrange goal to an immediate plan of action. We've gone from three years down the road and backtracked to the end of the current year and so on, to the third, second, and first quarters—creating a chronological list of stepping-stones that will ultimately result in the accomplishment of your three-year goals.

STEP #6: LIST AVAILABLE RESOURCES

Next, write down all the resources available to you to help you reach your three-year goals. Who or what could assist you? What books, CDs, mentors, coaches, seminars, information, technology, or other resources could you employ to accomplish your goals? Identify the organizations and groups with which you might need to create strategic alliances.

STEP #7: LIST POTENTIAL OBSTACLES

Now that you've written down all the potential resources, take a moment to think about what could prevent you from reaching your goals. Do you have any habits, attitudes, or beliefs that may hinder your progress? How will you personally need to change and grow before this goal can be reached? What about your finances? What about undeveloped skills? Have you mastered the vital skill of time management? What else could keep you from reaching this goal? What might go wrong?

List all the possible obstacles you may encounter. Think of this as contingency preparation or crisis-anticipation planning, and include anything that may hinder you in reaching a goal. This may seem pessimistic, but obstacles aren't necessarily negative. It depends on how you interpret them and what you do with them. If you write down the obstacles and take a good look at each one,

> Envision yourself having accomplished your goals. Stand on the mountaintop and look down at where you have been. Observe what you have achieved to reach your goal. What was the last step you took? Write that down. The next-to-last step? Write that too. Retrace your steps back down the mountain, writing all the way. The words you write will become your landmarks as you climb the mountain in reality and achieve your goals.

you often find many don't even exist. And other obstacles that loom huge in your mind tend to shrink when they're written on paper.

Obstacles build your goal-achieving muscles. They hold the raw materials of exciting opportunities. Any major or worthwhile goal has barriers. If it doesn't, it's not even really a goal—it's simply busywork and won't bring many rewards.

STEP #8: IDENTIFY WAYS TO OVERCOME OBSTACLES

The next step is to list some solutions to help you overcome the obstacles you just wrote down. Look at each obstacle as a problem waiting to be solved, and approach each one assuming that you already have a good solution. Though we may not realize it, we frequently come face-to-face with the exact obstacle we need at just the right time to sharpen us where we need it the most. All challenges, if dealt with directly and swiftly, will make us stronger, better, and wiser.

Remember, your ninety-day milestones lead to the accomplishment of your three-year goals.

Challenges and setbacks are intended to teach us something. They prepare us to perform more effectively at the next level. Just as it's necessary to bench-press 150 pounds before you try 200 pounds, it's also necessary to overcome obstacles along the path to your goals. And the more ambitious you are, the more challenges will be thrown your way. Again, many times great opportunities arise when you encounter obstacles, and these opportunities become more apparent when you maintain a positive, resourceful attitude and when you take time to analyze the situation in a relaxed state of mind. To paraphrase Booker T. Washington, success is not measured so much by our accomplishments in life but by what we had to overcome in the process. Keep in mind that we are goal-striving organisms. We're engineered to solve problems, and we function best and are happiest when we're moving toward a goal.

FOLLOWING THROUGH AFTER THE WORKSHOP

To implement and coordinate a concrete system for keeping up with your goal-directed activities, use three lists: First, maintain a quarterly strategy list of everything you must do to accomplish each of your ninety-day milestones. From that, select the most important items to create your weekly objectives or weekly master list. Next, plan each

Dear brothers and sisters, when troubles come your way, consider it an opportunity for great joy. For you know that when your faith is tested, your endurance has a chance to grow. *(James 1:2-3, NLT)*

day from your weekly list. As a result, you move from a long, quarterly strategy list to a weekly master list to a few manageable items for each day—all leading you toward your three-year vision.

Lesson 3 Questions for Reflection

In what areas of your life have you grown the most over the past ten years?

In what areas of your life have you grown the least in the past ten years?

Why do you think goals aren't emphasized more in school or church?

What could be the benefits of introducing your kids to goal setting early in life?

How do you envision that a marriage could be strengthened through goal setting?

———— ∞ ————

Whom can you influence with the ideas from this lesson in the next forty-eight hours?

LESSON 3 ASSIGNMENTS

1 │ Brainstorm 150 goals for the next thirty years of your life, and write them down.

2 │ Choose five goals to focus on for the next three years. Make sure you have a well-balanced set of goals.

3 │ Using the "back from the future" technique, plan on paper how you will accomplish your goals.

4 │ Begin the powerful habit of rewriting your top five goals each morning.

Choose to Invest Your Time Wisely

You can't make more time,

only better choices.

In this lesson, you will learn to

- **Minimize wasted time**

- **Work smarter**

- **Reduce stress**

- **Stay organized**

- **Experience inner peace**

- **Put into practice twenty-one**
  time-savers

The pages that follow provide powerful, usable, and highly effective time-management strategies that have had a dramatic effect on the lives of my clients in The 1% Club, as well as for countless other highly successful individuals.

In some instances, you will be able to implement these ideas immediately. At other times, you may not yet be in a position to put these tactics into practice. Fortunately, you can approach the following ideas like you would an enormous dinner buffet. Just as you would not—or at least should not—eat everything on the buffet, it's neither necessary nor recommended that you try to apply every single tactic we discuss in this chapter. I'd like you to concentrate on the most "nutritious" and most overlooked portion of time management, which is what I call Vital Time. These are the activities that are often squeezed out of your schedule by the addictive urgency of daily living. It's been said that all behavior is an expression of one's character. When you begin putting some of these recommendations into practice, it will free you to engage in Vital Time, which in turn allows you to express who you are and what you believe in. **Remember, the intent of time management is to enhance the quality and balance of your life, not simply to speed it up!**

If you want to minimize wasted time, work smarter, maximize your productive capabilities, and experience more Vital Time, then this lesson is for you. If you want to work less but earn even more, this lesson is for you. These pages contain practical ideas and techniques.

Each strategy presented has been field-tested and proven to be workable in the challenging arena of modern living. In fact, many of the techniques you're about to learn I put into practice to complete this book. After finishing this project, which required countless hours of research, writing, editing, and even more editing (and which had to be done around my previous commitments and already full schedule), I'm more convinced than ever of the validity of the

Rapid-Fire Time-Saver #1

Communicate to every employee what five minutes of wasted time means on a company-wide yearly scale. Relate those numbers to profits and salaries.

ideas I'm about to share with you. They are evidence of my personal triumph over procrastination and the other real and imagined diversions that hold most people back. By consistently and diligently applying these principles, you'll have more time for yourself, your family, and your friends.

With the other chapters in this book, I recommend that you read from start to finish, capturing the full scope of the principles I've presented, answering the questions, and completing the assignments. In this chapter, I encourage you to browse, reviewing the bold headers and selecting the sections that seem most relevant and important to you given where you are in life right now and especially in light of where you want to be in the future. This chapter was written not just to equip you but also to challenge you to raise the bar in your own life. Though you may not be able to put every recommendation (such as delegation) into practice, there is something (such as overcoming procrastination) in this chapter for everyone, and that includes you. As you progress through the upcoming pages, continually ask yourself, "How could I use this principle? How could this work for me right now? How could I become a more effective steward of my time?"

What Is Time?

Time is a unique resource—invisible, unalterable, and unstoppable. Everyone has the same amount of time. You and I must live on 86,400 seconds, 1,440 minutes, or 24 hours each day. That's 168 hours a week, approximately 720 hours per month, 8,640 hours per year, 177,800 hours over the next twenty years, and about 691,200 hours in a lifetime if a person lives to be eighty. And each segment of time we receive must be spent instantly.

Before we go any further, let me point out that human nature is the great archrival of personal effectiveness. I routinely conduct time-management workshops and seminars for large and small organizations in a wide variety of industries. Inevitably, no matter who my audience happens to be, I hear these same cries:

- "But our situation is unique."

- "Our business is such that it's impossible to properly plan, delegate, organize, hold effective meetings, or otherwise practice solid, proven, time-management habits."

- "That won't work for us because . . ."

Nonsense! Let me translate what these naysayers really mean: "Due to the nature of our particular business, we're forced to operate inefficiently." Think about that for a second. "Due to the nature of our particular business, we're forced to operate inefficiently." Doesn't that sound a bit crazy?

The common thread to these comments is none other than human nature. All human beings have a natural inclination to resist change, and nothing is quite as challenging as changing a bad or self-defeating habit. We want our lives and businesses to improve, but sometimes not quite enough that we are willing to change. But remember this: If any area of your life is to get better, you must get better. This means you must be willing to replace sloppy habits with the habits of success and peak performance. Aristotle reminded us thousands of years ago that "We are what we repeatedly do." And if you're committed to repeatedly applying the principles in this lesson, you will be amazed by the difference!

Don't fall into the trap of thinking that your time constraints are unique and unmanageable. It doesn't matter where or how you're currently living. You might live in the projects or in a mansion on the hill or anywhere in between, but one thing remains constant: **No matter who you are, your progress and success in life will depend, more than any other factor, on how you invest the twenty-four hours you're blessed with each day.** In fact, contrary to popular belief, it's not just the most talented, gifted, well-educated, affluent, or advantaged people

Rapid-Fire Time-Saver #2

Consider finding a convenient hideaway where you can isolate yourself. It can be in the building you work in, at home, close to your home, or even in your car, parked in a quiet place.

who achieve outstanding results in life. Nor is it the most intelligent, the hardest working, or the most creative. Success in life comes from one thing: deciding exactly what you want to accomplish and then deliberately choosing to invest the minutes and hours of your life doing only those things that move you in the direction of your goals. This lesson will give you the street smarts to do just that.

If you're willing to seize the initiative, you can learn time management just like you can learn to use a computer, play a sport, or any other skill you desire to master. The more ambitious you are, the better you must be at squeezing every last bit of usefulness out of every minute at your disposal. If you don't make the most out of an hour or even a minute, you'll never get a second chance. Remember, whether or not you want to admit it, many people are even busier than you are, but they accomplish more hour to hour, day to day. They obviously don't have more time. They just put their time to greater advantage. And you can do that as well!

> Vital Time is the quantity of time you invest in principle-based, goal-directed activities.

Your Self-Image Affects the Way You Manage Time

To create Vital Time, you must understand how your internal picture of yourself affects your ability to make the best use of your life. Your self-image affects how well you spend your time because when you believe you can manage your time well, you feel in control rather than as though you're simply reacting to external pressures. You have the ability to organize the events of your life so they make sense. The first step to becoming someone in control, someone who is an outstanding manager of his or her time, is to explore and improve your self-image.

Formed primarily from your environment, your self-image is the subconscious mechanism responsible for guiding your behavior. **We always act consistently with the image we have of ourselves.** If you see yourself as someone who is overly busy with far too many things to do, someone who is disorganized or working too hard, then your attempt to master your time will be in vain. Your weak self-image handcuffs your abilities and hampers your efforts at controlling your time. In fact, you cannot expect to behave differently from your self-image programming any more than you can expect to put a chocolate cake in the oven and an hour later take out an apple pie. You get out only what you put in.

Your self-image regulates your behavior just like a thermostat controls the room temperature. It determines how you use your time, knowledge, skills, and experiences. And far too often, we don't question the validity of our self-image. We simply behave as if it were true.

The key to becoming an outstanding time manager is to start thinking and speaking of yourself as an outstanding time manager. For example, if someone asks you about your day, you might say, "Today is the best day I've ever had. I've managed my time perfectly today. I don't have time to tell you any more now because I've got things to do." Vocalize, verbalize, and then actualize.

Changing your terminology changes your self-image. Changing your self-image changes your attitude. And changing your attitude changes your actions. I often like to say, "Attitude outranks facts." To develop the right attitude, ask yourself, "How would I act if I were already an excellent time manager? How would I act if I were the most effective time manager in the world?"

Imagine that someone offered you fifty thousand dollars to play the part of an excellent time manager in a movie. What are some of the things you would do? Well, you would sit up straight; you'd have your desk organized. You would move quickly. You'd work on one thing at a time and work from a list. You would check your e-mail proactively and on schedule. You'd anticipate and plan for interruptions. As Hamlet says, "Assume a virtue, if you have it not."[1] If you start acting like an excellent time manager, really pretending you're already a model of personal effectiveness,

Rapid-Fire Time-Saver #3

During breaks in the workday or when you are coming and going, use the stairs. It's a great way to maximize your time and burn extra calories.

the habits will lock in like a vise. Soon you will become an excellent time manager in reality.

The Time of Your Life

There is always enough time to achieve what God wants you to accomplish. That advice was drilled into me early in my life. It's a bit blunt, but it expresses a great truth. There is never enough time to do everything, but there is enough time to do the right things. Determining what the few right things are can be a bit challenging, especially when we are surrounded by an avalanche of short-term cultural trends and suggestions. The noise of modern society can subtly distract and divert even the most committed among us. One of the most curious aspects of human nature is that we will fail to find time to proactively set clear priorities, yet we will squander even more time reactively dealing with the inevitable messes created by such neglect. Are you living deliberately right now? That question is what time management is all about.

As we touched on in lesson 1, you tend to make wise decisions when you take into account the longest time horizon. When you consider an opportunity and ask, "I wonder how this will affect me in the next ten years, twenty years, or even longer," you tend to be very satisfied with your decisions. On the other hand, your biggest regrets often originate when you factor in only a short span of time, such as a year, month, week, or even the next fifteen minutes. Reflect for a moment on the choices you'd love to buy back, if you could, that were facilitated by a short-time perspective. Breaches of integrity are close neighbors with short-term thinking. Rarely will character break down when the long-term consequences are sufficiently weighed. After choosing a long-term perspective, it's critical to surround yourself with other individuals who share your strong commitment to the same priorities. Over time, and sometimes rather quickly, we take on the

Rapid-Fire Time-Saver #4

Measure your time in small increments, such as fifteen minutes. Attorneys do it, after all. It creates awareness, speed, and momentum.

"I Didn't Have Time"

It has been said that four simple words characterize mediocrity most accurately: *"I didn't have time."* Neither you nor anyone else could have a more damaging excuse concerning success. When you tell someone that you didn't have time, you simply reinforce their perception of you as someone who can't be relied on to get the job done. And when you tell yourself that you didn't have enough time, you undermine your inner credibility and fortify a self-image of underachievement and irresponsibility.

values, habits, and attitudes of the people with whom we spend most of our time. If your friends and coworkers compromise on matters that are important to you, it's only a matter of time before you become similarly influenced. With whom are you investing most of your time . . . and are they moving you in the direction of your full potential?

We all know where good intentions are likely to take us. There is a certain, well-traveled road that is paved with them. Pleasant intentions and other good thoughts are only a starting point, a commencement, not a finish line. Besides, most of us entertain worthwhile intentions. That's not the problem. The question is whether or not you have altered the way you use your time to fulfill those intentions. How have you positioned yourself to keep your promises and honor your commitments? Have you set yourself up for likely success, or have you weakened your probability of living in alignment with what's most important? Take a moment to scan your life and determine your priorities. What are the top five priorities in your life and how are they ordered? Do you put your work before your health? Do you put your kids before your marriage? Do you allow busyness to crowd out time with God? Do you ask yourself questions like this on a frequent basis? What are the long-term consequences of placing your priorities in the wrong order?

Rapid-Fire Time-Saver #5

If you have a separate set of keys for each set of locks, you're likely to end up at the right lock with the wrong keys! Prepare a complete set of all your important keys, and then make as many duplicate sets as necessary. Then, no matter which set you pick up, you will never be locked out of your home, your office, or the car you choose to drive. Always leave your keys in the same spot so you can find them quickly.

The Power of 15

What could you do to enhance your life if you had an extra fifteen minutes each day? You might want to read something uplifting or maybe review your most important goals. You might want to stretch your lower back or take a quick walk. Maybe you'd turn this extra fifteen minutes into prayer or journaling time. Perhaps this bonus time could be used to chip away at an overwhelming clutter project or to better plan the next day. You might play a quick game with your kids or write a note to a special friend. If you give it some thought, just fifteen minutes a day can change your life. I'm confident you can find this "extra" fifteen minutes somewhere in your day. Consider cutting fifteen minutes of daily television or newspaper time and reallocating it to a higher priority activity. Or consider waking up just fifteen minutes earlier or staying up fifteen minutes later. Possibly you could shave fifteen minutes off your lunch routine. If you look for this extra fifteen minutes, you'll find it. I challenge you to re-budget just fifteen minutes a day, seven days a week, to an activity of higher value. Three months from now, those fifteen extra minutes will accumulate to 22.5 bonus hours. And three years from now, those fifteen short minutes will add up to more than eleven extra twenty-four-hour days, or thirty extra nine-hour days. Fortunately, you already have these extra days, but how will you choose to invest them? It's worth thinking about because it is the time of your life!

Ten Recommendations

No matter where you are in life or what restrictions you have on how you use your time, the following ten recommendations will help you live on-purpose and make the most of the twenty-four hours you receive each day.

1 | **Know your life goals.** We covered this in lesson 3, but it is worth pointing out that nothing wastes more time than not having a set of clear goals for your life, for the year, for the week, and for the day.

2 | **Make a priority "to do" list each evening for the following day.** You'll sleep better, wake up with more enthusiasm, and be a better steward of your time all day long.

3 | **Wake up early, before the time when your obligations and responsibilities kick in.** Organize your bed

time and wake-up time so that you have at least fifteen to thirty minutes to yourself before you have to get dressed, deal with the kids, or leave for work. A morning buffer time puts you, not frenetic circumstances, in charge of your day.

4 | **Return as many of your phone calls and e-mails as possible at one or two predetermined times during the day.** This will save most people from twenty to thirty minutes a day that would ordinarily be wasted. We'll discuss this from a business standpoint a little later in the chapter.

5 | **Batch or group as many of your daily or weekly errands as possible** so that time is not lost by simple inefficiency.

6 | **Think of your relationships as precious investments.** I've observed in my coaching experience that nothing can compete with the regret caused by looking back and realizing, "I've spent way too much time with the wrong people." In light of God's purpose for your life, are you investing enough time with the right relationships?

7 | **Avoid the quick-fix mind-set at all costs!** Instead, do it right the first time. If you don't have time to do it in excellent fashion the first time, when will you have time to do it over? Taking shortcuts saves time today, but it costs even more time in the future.

8 | **Thoughtfully prune something in your life each year, or maybe even every quarter.** Abandon as quickly and politely as possible those obligations, projects, habits,

and commitments that you've come to realize no longer serve your God-given purpose. Big or small, what could you let go of today and never even miss?

9 | **Insulate yourself sufficiently from distractions.** You will be far more effective as a mom, dad, husband, wife, or business partner if you routinely have some space or margin where you can quietly think and proactively take care of yourself without being interrupted by others. Then, schedule time daily or weekly to deal with the important people, projects, and priorities in your life.

10 | **Constantly remind yourself that time equals life!** View each hour of the day as a gift. Stay aware of your time like a world-class athlete watches his or her diet. Quickly evaluate each day in less than two minutes by asking, "What went well today? What didn't go very well? What will I do differently tomorrow?"

Remember, your ability to manage your time affects your marriage, your parenting, your fitness, and your potential for influence in the marketplace.

Vital Time Tactics

The following ten tactics will help you manage your work responsibilities more efficiently. As a result, you will be able to enjoy more Vital Time. In fact, the aim of this entire chapter is to help you create more Vital Time, at work and especially at home. In my life, for example, I am continuously striving to increase the time I invest with my top clients, the time I invest creating and delivering content, and the time I

Rapid-Fire Time-Saver #6

Compile commonly sought materials into binders or digital files, or create digital shortcuts to them. You'll avoid sorting through files to retrieve the answers to frequently asked questions.

invest thinking strategically about my coaching practice. At home, my Vital Time includes quiet time each morning, physical exercise, uninterrupted time with my wife, and quantity time with my three sons. What about you? What do you consider your Vital Time?

VITAL TIME TACTIC #1: OVERCOME PROCRASTINATION

You must win the battle against procrastination to rise above the average and create Vital Time. If beating procrastination were not one of your objectives, you probably would not be reading this book. Peak performance and procrastination are simply incompatible. It is certainly accurate that "tomorrow" can only be found in the calendar of fools.

Procrastination, which means delaying higher-priority tasks in favor of lower-priority ones, is responsible for more frustration, stress, and underachievement than any other single factor. It is the art of keeping up with yesterday and avoiding today. Procrastination causes emotional anguish, devastates personal relationships, wrecks any attempt at effectiveness, and promotes physical and mental exhaustion. Procrastination is all about excuses, and you know as well as I do that the excuses you have today are the excuses you will have tomorrow. Today's excuses are but the ancestors to tomorrow's excuses and the predecessors to future mediocrity.

So how can you defeat procrastination and start creating Vital Time? Most often the hardest part of getting started is getting started. Once you're involved, you've overcome the highest hurdle. And you don't always have to start at the beginning. If the first step seems hard or too large, start with another part of the project. Or set a minigoal, such as working at something for fifteen minutes, whether it's reading, exercising, or a work project. Often after fifteen minutes you'll want to continue. You may even complete the entire task. I used a kitchen timer, set for fifteen minutes, to get me in the habit of daily reading. I usually ended up reading much longer, and that habit is now ingrained as a part of my

Rapid-Fire Time-Saver #7

Schedule your most difficult tasks during your most productive time of the day.

Seven Ways to Procrastinate Effectively

———————— *A Parody* ————————

1 | Just wish, hope, and dream. There's really no need to set clear, specific goals and then roll up your sleeves and get to work.

2 | Always work on what's fun and easy—C and B tasks—rather than doing A priorities—the things that are often hard but necessary. Don't low-priority tasks build momentum?

3 | Stay in your career even if you find yourself unhappy, stuck, and unable to grow. You can always look forward to the evenings and weekends.

4 | Always delay difficult work if you're tired! Use fatigue strategically to escape those uncomfortable tasks.

5 | If you fear something is wrong with you physically, don't see a doctor. That way you can avoid dealing with the reality of a possible illness. It's much easier to wait until you're really sick.

6 | Tomorrow is always a good day to start something important, such as exercising or dieting. Next week is even better.

7 | Take a break from all projects when you hit the 90 percent completion mark. That way you'll always have them to come back to.

daily routine. Break large jobs down into small pieces or daily doables. As the saying goes, "How do you eat an elephant? Piece by piece, one bite at a time."

Develop a sense of urgency, a "do it now" attitude, a bias for action. And use a fast tempo. The faster you are, the more productive you'll be. Believe it or not, you'll get less fatigued walking fast, doing things fast, and getting out and moving than you will if you're trudging around.

Learn to make decisions quickly as well. Successful people take little time to make a decision and a long time to change a decision once it has been made. Good decision making involves anticipating what the options are and assessing the pluses and minuses of each one. Develop a system that you use consistently when making decisions. Get input from good decision makers and learn from them. And remember, it's better to make a bad decision than to make no decision at all. Making no decision produces stagnation and triggers feelings of failure, confusion, and worry. It's been said that even the best plans fall flat if you're consumed by indecision and make no move to put a plan into action. Be a doer, not a wisher or a hoper.

If your life is to get better, you have to do something constructive to make it better. There's nothing more constructive than eliminating procrastination from your life.

VITAL TIME TACTIC #2: ORGANIZE YOUR WORK SPACE

You must have a strategically organized work space. You can practice all the other time-management principles, but if you remain disorganized, you're going to severely restrict the effectiveness of the other principles you practice. **Most disorganization comes from indecision**—for example, not being able to decide if a piece of paper or some other information is important, and if it is, what to do with it. This is manifested in

Rapid-Fire Time-Saver #8

If you make an appointment well in advance, call the day before to confirm, asking for a response only if plans have changed. This is professional, and it saves time and embarrassment.

Seven Valid Reasons to Procrastinate

A Parody

1 | Most obviously, putting things off allows you to escape from unpleasant activities. These could be things that you're afraid to do or simply things that you don't enjoy doing.

2 | If you wait for things to get better, you can still blame the world for your unhappiness. Enough of that personal responsibility stuff.

3 | You can subtly manipulate others to do the job. If you put it off long enough, somebody else eventually may have to step in and do it for you.

4 | You can avoid the increased responsibility that goes with success. If you do a job well and on time, others will only expect you to do it again. This, of course, is grossly unfair.

5 | If you don't feel like doing the job now, you can plan to do it later. Some call this laziness, but they're rude.

6 | You can claim perfectionist immunity. Because you're so conscientious, others will understand if you never get started.

7 | If you're not sure, wait. This is a good rule of thumb. A difficult, overwhelming, or insurmountable task should always be delayed until you're absolutely ready and well rested.

the habit of picking up the same things three or four times, having a constantly overstuffed in-box, and having multiple stacks of papers, periodicals, and files lying around the office. If your office is typical, roughly three-quarters of the items in your files should be deleted or placed in the trash.

On and around your work space, divide all objects into one of two categories: tools or supplies. Tools are reusable items like the stapler, telephone, tape holder, scissors, and letter openers. Supplies are consumable items such as staples, tape, correction

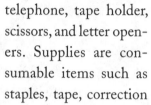

Successful people have successful habits. Mediocre people have mediocre habits. And it all starts with a choice.

fluid, paper clips, Post-it notes, and letterheads. Keep tools and supplies in a separate storage area, such as a drawer, on a shelf, or in cabinets.

Use an in-box and out-box. Check the boxes at least twice daily at specific, predetermined times. Appropriately file or act upon all incoming materials immediately. To maximize your effectiveness and productivity, avoid handling any item more than once. Another idea is to stand up as you sort your in-box; you'll move faster and save even more time.

Every time something comes to your desk or your e-mail in-box, ask, "Is it an action?" In other words, is it a to-do item? Is there some specific action you must take, or is it a support, a reference, or some sort of information that you may need to access sometime later? If it's something you may need to access later, put it in the appropriate file category and then alphabetize the information in that file. If it's an action or to-do, place it in one of three action categories:

- The routine to-do files if it's a recurring, routine task such as "to read," "write letters," or "call back"

- The priority to-do files if it's a task that must be prioritized

- The tickler to-do files if the task needs to be completed on a specific future date

I handle my incoming e-mail similarly to the way I handle physical items. I usually check my e-mail at designated times, typically second thing in the morning, before lunch, and before I leave the office in the early evening. I skim the new messages, quickly replying to any that I can handle in one hundred seconds or less and moving the rest to one of three subfolders. If I need to draft a significant reply or do something in response to the e-mail, I move it to the Action folder. If I need to review something, I move it to the Read/Review folder. If I need to wait on a response from someone else, I move the message to the Pending folder. I also move e-mails I have sent to the Pending folder if I must await a reply from someone. By default, all other e-mails are either deleted or saved by my assistant to our reference or research folders on our company server. Many of my 1% Club clients have adopted this simple system. You can set up a system like this for your home computer as well. I encourage you to try this approach or modify it a bit so it works well for you. E-mail can be a big time waster, so make sure you have a system that makes this part of your life easier.

Let's come back to filing paper now. My best advice is to categorize everything. Use hanging files, and consider not wasting time by placing manila file folders inside hanging file folders. Color code your hanging files by category using colored files, tabs, or both. The category should be indicated by a colored tab at the far left, followed by staggered, co-ordinating tabs for the related subjects and topics in each category. For example, "marketing" might be the category, "direct mail" might be the subject, "catalog" might be the topic, and the number, title, or item might be the "Summer 2008 issue" of the catalog.

Outline your color system in a word-processing document, and save it digitally for easy reference in the event that your assistant, another coworker, or a family member must access the files. For example, purple might be action files; green, client files; blue, research and reference; yellow, admin-istrative; and red, marketing. Document the color choices,

Rapid-Fire Time-Saver #9

Respond to mail by telephone or e-mail when you can. If possible, delegate this task.

and then create an index or a table of contents listing the files in each category. Update this index regularly. This takes a little time up front but saves time in the long run.

Next, a messy, disorganized desk will weigh you down. In fact, according to what I call the Principle of Correspondence, your outer life is a mirror image of your inner life. Everything you say and do, including your level of organization, is a reflection of the real you! If you constantly have a cluttered work area, it's a sign that you've got stress and turmoil going on inside that needs to be dealt with. The simple act of cleaning up your work area can make you feel more in control of your life and can help you be more effective, more efficient, and more optimistic. Often as you go higher and higher in organizations, the desks get cleaner and cleaner. And that's no coincidence.

Most importantly, the cleaner your work area and the fewer things on your desk, the more you will get done. Consider investing in a high-quality scanner and losing most of the paper. You can apply the same organizing principles and categories described above to your computer files as well.

VITAL TIME TACTIC #3: HANDLE READING MATERIAL MORE EFFICIENTLY

To be effective in today's rapidly changing society, you must stay up on current events and developments in your industry. Following are three keys to handling reading material:

First, become a speed-reader. A course in speed-reading will enable you to double or triple your reading speed almost instantly. I more than doubled my speed in the first two hours. Online courses are available, as well as seminars and CD learning systems. Courses in PhotoReading and accelerated learning are proven approaches you may also want to investigate. The remarkable results you get from practicing these simple methods will surprise you.

Another way to accelerate

Rapid-Fire Time-Saver #10

Develop a mastermind group of success-minded people who can accelerate your progress toward your goals.

your reading is to go straight to a book's table of contents, decide which chapter is most important to you, and then read that chapter or mark it for future reference. You may find that the material is not even worth reading, which of course shortens the allotted time considerably.

For business information, read only top-priority articles in magazines, publications, journals, newsletters, and so on. Again, read the table of contents, pick the items that are of the most interest to you, go right to those items, tear out the pages, and put the pages in your "to read" file. Then throw the rest of the magazine away. I recommend that you always take that file with you to read during what I call transition time—when you're waiting for an appointment, standing in line, or traveling. Train yourself to read only what's most important to you, nothing else. If you're fortunate enough to have an assistant, ideally you want to go through the table of contents, circle what's of interest to you, and ask your assistant to tear out the pages, put them in a file, and shove them into your hands on the way out of the office. Also, whenever you're reading or reviewing correspondence, stand up! Your mind will stay more focused and alert, and you'll get done much faster.

You may want to take advantage of services that provide a synopsis or overview of various books and articles. Written and audio summaries are available, as well as podcasts. I've made use of these for many years now and have cut out four or five hours of reading each week.

VITAL TIME TACTIC #4: HANDLE EVERYTHING ONCE AND ONLY ONCE
Single handling means that once you start a top-priority task, you stay with it until it's 100 percent complete. Persevere without diversion or distraction. Don't pick up the same task, the same piece of paper, or even the same phone call twice. Pick it up, swarm all over it, take care of it, then bring it to a close and go on to the next one.

Become a "monomaniac," as Peter Drucker called it. Learn to

Rapid-Fire Time-Saver #11

Because you absorb the habits of those you spend time with, associate only with time-conscious people. Stay away from negative people.

focus intensely on just one thing at a time because the more you take on, the greater the chance that you'll lose some of your effectiveness. This is true not only for a particular task but in all areas of your life. Research shows that great accomplishments require single-minded concentration. Review great success stories, and you'll see what I mean!

VITAL TIME TACTIC #5: DELEGATE

Delegation is the only way you can carve out enough Vital Time to pursue those things that are meaningful to you. Without delegation, you will end up with so many responsibilities that you can't do what matters most. Remember, focus on what you do best! As an entrepreneur, an executive, or a manager, you must delegate everything you possibly can to have enough time to complete your highest payback tasks. Delegate, and you'll free yourself from mundane tasks that don't move you closer to your goals.

The first step is to know when to delegate. A general rule of thumb is, if someone else can do the job faster, better, or more economically than you can, ask them to do it! **Direct increasing amounts of time to those aspects of your business for which you have the most passion and where you excel.** This is the prescription for exceptional success no matter what you do.

It's been said that activities that don't directly advance your goals and dreams are simply routine maintenance. And routine maintenance—while critical to the functioning of a house, a car, or any piece of machinery—can be performed by anyone who has the necessary skills. In other words, by a repair person or a handyman, or someone other than yourself. Unless your goal is to be a maid, butler, home-improvement expert, or auto mechanic, you may be sacrificing hundreds of hours

Rapid-Fire Time-Saver #12

Keep old-fashioned three-by-five-inch index cards or a mini digital recorder with you all the time for capturing great ideas and dictating correspondence. I use a dictation service that I can speed-dial from my mobile phone and then receive transcriptions rapidly by e-mail.

Use the Extra Time You've Freed Up to

- spend quantity and quality time with those you love

- work on important business and career goals and plans

- simply rest, relax, and rejuvenate

per year on activities that are not in alignment with your values nor contribute directly to the accomplishment of a single objective, goal, or dream.

You can't be goal directed and maintenance directed at the same time, so you must make a choice. However, if routine home and yard maintenance are enjoyable for you, then by all means do those tasks! These activities can be effective stress reducers and can also give you a sense of

Rapid-Fire Time-Saver #13

Call ahead or e-mail lunch orders to avoid waiting in line for take-out orders.

accomplishment. But if they're not your idea of a good time, delegate them.

The point here is that you can make the decision when to hire someone to take care of the chores you consider mundane maintenance. What you choose to delegate may be very different from what your neighbor or coworker chooses to delegate. The important thing is that you delegate those activities that drain your energy and obscure your focus.

It's important to decide not only *when* to delegate but *what* to delegate. Giving subordinates jobs that neither you nor anyone else wants to do isn't delegating, it's assigning. And although it's necessary at times, it doesn't nourish others' egos, encourage them to grow, or enable them to assume the decision-making role that can help to free more of your time. So learn to delegate challenging and rewarding tasks as well.

The next important step is to know *to whom* to delegate. My advice is to choose the best people available, no matter the cost. The best people will make you successful. They also cut down on the number of times you are interrupted because they know how to handle challenges themselves. The sooner you stop the interruptions in the office, the sooner you'll be living your life your way, on your terms, and fulfilling your goals. Remember that someone is always out there with the passion and knack for what you hope to avoid doing. Your job is to attract and recruit them.

Knowing when to delegate, to whom to delegate, and how to delegate will come more naturally with practice. You can rest assured it will put you well on your way to claiming and enjoying Vital Time.

Rapid-Fire Time-Saver #14

Avoid the herd. Do things when nobody else does them. Check out of your hotel at times when other people aren't. Dine out before crowds arrive. Schedule flights for nonpeak hours. Drive during nonpeak hours.

VITAL TIME TACTIC #6:
CONTROL YOUR PHONE CALLS
Control the phone, or it will control you and limit your level of accomplishment. Don't be afraid to ignore it completely if you're engaged in a vital activity. Voice-mail systems are cost effective and efficient at handling

Minimize Telephone Mediocrity

1 | Before you call, jot down the points you want to cover.

2 | Be prepared to cut off the conversation quickly by acknowledging how busy you know the other person is.

3 | Do easy, mindless jobs while on the phone, such as signing letters or organizing your desk.

4 | When possible, check your messages and return all necessary calls at the same time. Limit phone usage to a couple of specific periods during the day. You'll immediately become aware of the extra time and mental energy this frees up.

5 | Practice the phone-management Golden Rule: When you call someone else, value their time by asking, "Is this a good time?" Don't assume they have time to talk to you, and never interrupt simply because you want to chat!

messages. If you're fortunate enough to have an assistant, have your calls screened and get a specific call-back time when the caller will be in the office. When you call someone, leave a call-back time as well. Stop phone tag. Refuse to be a slave to the phone.

Another way to control the phone is to become the caller instead of the callee. Research indicates that unplanned phone calls last five to seven minutes longer than planned calls. If you make or receive twelve unplanned calls in a day, you might be wasting an hour. I have all my incoming calls carefully screened. That does occasionally irritate some people, which warns me that the offended party might be the type of person who can afford to waste time. In my office, under no circumstances are calls put through to me unless the caller fully identifies herself or himself and the reasons for calling. My staff also encourages callers to e-mail a brief introductory note before trying to reach me on the phone. Often a phone call is not needed at all.

VITAL TIME TACTIC #7: MANAGE INTERRUPTIONS

You must become exceptionally skilled at handling interruptions because they tend to be the number-one time waster in business. Remember, interruptions are usually people—people who want to refocus your attention from what you're doing now to something else. Some people just don't realize they're cutting into your time or disturbing your thought process, while others ramble on indefinitely, apparently believing they're getting paid by the word. They never seem to run out of inconsequential things to say. Sometimes, though, people genuinely need something from us that is a priority to them. How can we treat them with respect while still protecting our time? Here are some strategies for dealing with interruptions.

Adopt a controlled open-door policy, in which people have access to you but by appointment only. If you're a manager, develop your staff by requiring them,

Rapid-Fire Time-Saver #15

If you're having trouble making contact with someone for the first time on the telephone, consider faxing or e-mailing your message.

Manage Interruptions

Remember the value of an hour.

Look at your watch.

Schedule interruptions.

Hang a "do not disturb" sign.

Control your "open door."

"I'm on my way out."

Turn your desk away from the door.

"I only have eight minutes."

Remain standing.

before they bring you a problem, to define the problem clearly in writing, suggest three possible solutions, and then choose the best solution of the three. Often they'll determine there's no need to interrupt. And if they do interrupt, the length of disruption will be shortened. No one should be able to walk into your office without a good reason.

You could also designate specific times for interruptions and other times for no interruptions. Put a Do Not Disturb sign on your closed door during these uninterruptible periods, or move your work to a conference room or other quiet location. Make it absolutely clear that unless there's a death in the family or a fire in the building, you're not to be disturbed. During periods when you allow interruptions, engage in routine or operational tasks that can be easily returned to, not creative work.

When somebody unexpectedly drops in, consider standing up and beginning to leave. Say, "I'm on my way out," and hold the meeting right in your doorway. Then go to the restroom, down the hall, or whatever, and then get back to work.

Meet unexpected visitors in the reception area or lobby and remain standing if possible. Meet coworkers in their office rather than yours so you can get up and leave more easily when you feel the conversation is over.

Set time limits at the beginning of the discussion. If you have an unexpected guest, say, "I've only got seven minutes, then I have a phone appointment [or some other pressing business]." Using an unusual time frame commands attention and respect.

Discourage drop-in visitors by turning your desk away from the door. This eliminates eye contact with people walking by, which some interpret as an invitation for interruption. If someone does drop in, save time by writing a brief note to remind yourself where you left off.

Anxious body language shortens interruptions. Look at your watch, start to shuffle papers, look for something in your desk, or whatever you can

Rapid-Fire Time-Saver #16

Batch your errands. Do errands on one side of the street first, then on the other side on your way back.

Calculate the Value of an Hour

Total Annual Income	Total number of hours you work each week				
	30	40	50	60	70
	Approximate dollar value of an hour of your time				
$40,000	$26.67	$20.00	$16.00	$13.33	$11.43
$45,000	$30.00	$22.50	$18.00	$15.00	$12.86
$50,000	$33.33	$25.00	$20.00	$16.67	$14.29
$55,000	$36.67	$27.50	$22.00	$18.33	$15.71
$60,000	$40.00	$30.00	$24.00	$20.00	$17.14
$65,000	$43.33	$32.50	$26.00	$21.67	$18.57
$75,000	$50.00	$37.50	$30.00	$25.00	$21.43
$100,000	$66.67	$50.00	$40.00	$33.33	$28.57
$125,000	$83.33	$62.50	$50.00	$41.67	$35.71
$150,000	$100.00	$75.00	$60.00	$50.00	$42.86
$200,000	$133.33	$100.00	$80.00	$66.67	$57.14
$250,000	$166.67	$125.00	$100.00	$83.33	$71.43
$300,000	$200.00	$150.00	$120.00	$100.00	$85.71
$350,000	$233.33	$175.00	$140.00	$116.67	$100.00
$400,000	$266.67	$200.00	$160.00	$133.33	$114.29
$450,000	$300.00	$225.00	$180.00	$150.00	$128.57
$500,000	$333.33	$250.00	$200.00	$166.67	$142.86
$750,000	$500.00	$375.00	$300.00	$250.00	$214.29
$1,000,000	$666.67	$500.00	$400.00	$333.33	$285.71
Total Hours Worked Annually (50 weeks)	1,500	2,000	2,500	3,000	3,500

To calculate the dollar value of an hour of your time, divide your annual income by the number of hours you work each year.

One hour is worth: $_____

I want one hour to be worth: $_____

think of, and the hint will be received. I know some people who always have a mundane task that they ask drop-in visitors to help them with. The more tedious, the better. Again, they'll get the message.

If your assistant and staff are your most frequent interruptions, schedule regular blocks of time to meet and cover all problems and questions in one session.

Finally, remember that your time is valuable. Suppose, for example, that you want to earn $100,000 this year. That translates into approximately $50 an hour, or about 83 cents each minute. Keep this fresh in your mind—**most people who interrupt others have no clue as to the value of each minute of their time or yours!**

VITAL TIME TACTIC #8: GROUP SIMILAR TASKS

Do similar things together. Everything we do is subject to what is called the learning curve. When we do a series of five to ten similar tasks, the learning curve reduces the amount of time needed to complete each item by about 80 percent.

For instance, in running my business, it's much more productive for me to set aside certain days for client training, other days for product development, and other days for reviewing research, rather than doing a little bit here and a little bit there, having to mentally warm up to each type of activity each time. Batch your phone calls and correspondence as well. Do them all at once, and you can add about an hour to your day.

VITAL TIME TACTIC #9: BLOCK OUT CHUNKS OF TIME

You wouldn't believe the feedback I get from entrepreneurs and other leaders on the impact of time blocking. **The more important your work becomes, the more important it is for you to develop blocks of time where you can work on serious projects without distraction.** Avoid mixing creative tasks with functional or administrative tasks. In fact, it's

Rapid-Fire Time-Saver #17

If you travel a lot, keep a file in your car full of directions to places you might return to.

Mute the phone during lunch.	Block out three to four hours a day.

Schedule Quiet, Unbroken Time

Join the five o'clock club.	First-class travel pays.

impossible to maximize your personal effectiveness if you try to blend operational tasks—such as answering the phone, drafting correspondence, returning e-mails, and holding meetings—with creative projects—such as planning, crafting a proposal, or designing a new marketing campaign. You need blocks of time—minimum blocks of two or preferably three hours, on a regular basis. It takes about thirty to sixty minutes for your mind to get acclimated to creative tasks.

Here are several recommendations for scheduling quiet, unbroken time. Each will dramatically increase your effectiveness and produce the wellspring of creative ideas that come from uninterrupted thought.

Rapid-Fire Time-Saver #18

Avoid "bargainitis," which is the inflammation of the poverty gland. Bargainitis is simply the practice of false economy. Don't allow cost to be your only criteria. Smart buyers know that the concept of "penny-wise and pound-foolish" advocated by Ben Franklin still holds true.

First, start off in the morning when you are freshest and most alert. Join the five o'clock club and get up at 5 a.m. Work on important lifetime priorities, goals, and devotions early in the morning. Almost all great leaders are early risers. After working on personal development, you can devote the rest of your early-morning time to professional projects. This way you've had ninety minutes of uninterrupted time before you've even gone to the office. Or you can get into the office an hour or more earlier than anyone else. But even if you arrive at the office at the usual time, you've already accomplished ninety minutes of uninterrupted work.

Lunch is another excellent option for time blocking. From noon to 1 p.m., mute the telephone. While everyone else is gone, you can work uninterrupted for more than an hour, clearing up e-mail or tackling chunks of major projects.

Block off a set time every day. For instance, from ten a.m. to noon, put a Do Not Disturb sign on the outside of your office door, and for two hours, take no interruptions. If you do the same thing between two and four p.m., you'll get in a solid two hours in the morning and the afternoon. The exact times you do this don't really matter. Just do it!

Don't overlook travel as an opportunity for time blocking. One hour of flying first class, for example, can be the equivalent of about three hours of work in an office environment, because there aren't any interruptions. The first-class cabin is also an excellent venue for connecting with other success-minded individuals. It very likely could be worth the extra investment.

In The 1% Club, we have a concept called The DayBlock System, through which we teach entrepreneurs how to block out entire days—and in some cases,

Rapid-Fire Time-Saver #19

Experiment with tipping in advance. Remember what tip stands for: "to insure performance (or promptness)." If you're at a nice restaurant and in a hurry, simply tell the person who seats you that you're pressed for time and ask him if he can speed things up in the kitchen. Then slip a bill into his hand and repeat the same maneuver when the server comes. Also, tip generously at any restaurant you frequent. It's an investment!

Vital Time Tactics

1 | Overcome procrastination

2 | Organize your work space

3 | Handle reading material efficiently

4 | Handle everything once and only once

5 | Delegate

6 | Control your phone calls

7 | Manage interruptions

8 | Batch similar tasks

9 | Block out chunks of time

10 | Run masterful meetings

even weeks—as a focusing tool. For example, we divide each week into three types of days. The first type is called a Rejuvenation Day and is reserved for rest and recreation. The second type of day is called a SuperFocus Day, which is used exclusively for dealing with your top three highest-payback activities. The third type of day, called Prep Days, are used to handle clutter projects and to organize yourself so that you can be free of low-payback activities when you have a SuperFocus Day on the schedule. As members of The 1% Club gradually master this unique approach, they experience greater productivity as a result of eliminating recurring distractions and continually shifting back and forth between different mental gears.

VITAL TIME TACTIC #10: RUN MASTERFUL MEETINGS

How do your meetings measure up? Are they an investment or a waste of time? Here are six essential guidelines for effective meetings.

Know the purpose. Is the goal to solve a problem, to train employees, to share information, or to plan a project? Be able to define the purpose of the meeting in less than twenty-five words!

Is the meeting absolutely necessary? Or is there another way to accomplish the same result? Who must attend? What is the worst thing that could happen if the meeting were not held at all? Most meetings are big time wasters, so view all meetings as investments that should reap large dividends. Multiply the hourly wages of meeting attendees by the number of hours of the meeting to determine the true cost of the get-together.

Develop a written agenda. E-mail a copy of meeting topics to participants in advance of the meeting. List the items in order of importance to the organization. Begin the meeting with a one-sentence statement of purpose, then give a specific adjournment time.

Prepare! Prepare for the meeting as if it were a client presentation. Always do your

Rapid-Fire Time-Saver #20

Create checklists for recurring activities like home maintenance, car maintenance, house cleaning, vacation planning, and grocery shopping. You won't have to rethink them each time the need arises.

homework, and never waste attendees' time with tasks or dialogue that could be handled elsewhere.

Lead the meeting effectively. Keep the meeting on track and state the outcome of each point discussed. Close each point before moving on, and don't skip around. Assign all tasks and deadlines, including taking and distributing meeting minutes or notes. Determine how each task will be implemented and controlled. Be absolutely clear on what is to be done and why, and have employees restate the task, the deadline, and the purpose to make sure everyone understands what's going on. Above all, make decisions. Meetings without decisions are worthless.

Get out fast. If you are no longer necessary for the completion of the meeting, leave. Try to get items affecting you discussed first, and then leave and get back to work! Leaders should give their people permission to depart after their contribution has been made.

We all have just twenty-four hours each day to achieve our goals and to become the person we are capable of becoming. As I said at the beginning of this lesson, no matter who you are, your progress and ultimate success in life will depend more on what you do with the twenty-four hours you're given each day than on any other single factor. You can invest your time wisely or you can waste it foolishly. You can create Vital Time or you can let it slip away. The choice, as always, is yours. It's completely up to you!

Remember, each of us has massive room for improvement and advancement. Your output can be more than increased—it can be multiplied repeatedly. In fact, I believe you have an obligation to maximize every drop of your potential. And when you've risen to this next peak of supereffectiveness, you'll find it hard to believe you used to live any other way!

Rapid-Fire Time-Saver #21

Do things right the first time. If you don't have time to do it right the first time, when will you have time to redo it?

Lesson 4 Questions for Reflection

What is one area where you need to take action but have been procrastinating?

What impact could your time-management skills have on the quality of your home life? What are your children learning from observing how you use your time?

How much margin or unscheduled time do you need on a daily, weekly, and monthly basis to operate at your peak?

In what ways has technology influenced how you invest or spend your time (Internet, e-mail, mobile phones, iPods, etc.)?

What are the key activities that tend to create the biggest difference in your family life? at work? Which activities should definitely be pruned?

Whom can you influence with the ideas from this lesson in the next forty-eight hours?

LESSON 4 ASSIGNMENTS

1 | Determine how much your time is currently worth (see chart on page 119).

2 | Determine how much your time should be worth to create the lifestyle you desire.

3 | Make a list of your three highest payback activities, both personally and professionally.

4 | Keep a log of how you spend your time for the next two weeks. (Use fifteen-minute increments.)

5 | Based on this lesson, brainstorm a list of twenty specific ways you can improve your personal time management.

Choose to Get Out of Your Own Way

Whatever you direct your mind to think about will ultimately be revealed for everyone to see.

In this lesson, you will learn to

- Use the language of success
- Flush unwanted dialogue out of your mind
- Control your emotions
- Build beliefs that make success inevitable
- Get out of your own way
- Reprogram yourself for extraordinary accomplishment

Among the most powerful influences on your character, personality, and attitude is what you say to yourself and believe. During every single moment of every day, you are talking yourself either into or out of success. By talking yourself into success, I mean talking yourself into being the champion God designed you to become. Remember our discussion in lesson 2 about finding God's unique purpose for your life. With every thought that races through your mind, you are constantly redefining yourself and your future. **Your inner dialogue, or self-talk, can and must be effectively harnessed if you are to maximize your full potential.** Harnessing your self-talk doesn't require magic, just a deliberate effort to align your thought life with God's best plans for your life. It's training your mind via your mouth. Matthew 12:34 says, "Out of the overflow of the heart the mouth speaks" (NIV). Your words and mental images reflect what you believe in your heart—and if you change those words and images, you will also change your heart.

Breaking Out of the Cube

He's been on the cover of *Newsweek* and *Fortune,* appeared as the spokesperson for a multimillion-dollar company, and two books written about him have ranked number one on the *New York Times* best-sellers list. No, I'm not talking about Jack Welch or Bill Gates; I'm referring to Dilbert, the popular cartoon character created by Scott Adams, who humorously reminds everyday office workers that they are not alone in their frustration.

Adams has made a career of drawing out the humor in the typical office worker's life. His nationally syndicated comic strip appears in two thousand newspapers in sixty-five countries, making it one of the more successful comic strips in history.[1] Each year, devoted fans support the *Dilbert* merchandising empire by buying books, mouse pads, coffee mugs, and calendars.

So how did Adams break out of his routine engineering job at Pacific Bell to become a successful cartoonist? He used a process called affirmations, which he learned from a friend who had read a book on the subject. She had tried it out for herself and had success, and Adams figured he had nothing to lose. The process consisted of visualizing what he wanted and then writing down that goal fifteen times in a row, each day, until he obtained the thing he'd visualized.[2] Basically, he talked himself into being successful.

OUTSIDE HELP

Although Adams had been successful in school, graduating from high school as valedictorian and receiving a bachelor of arts in economics from Hartwick College, he had little knowledge about his desired profession. He wanted to be a cartoonist, but he had no idea how to get started.

In 1986, Adams took a significant step toward reaching his goal by contacting Jack Cassady, the host of a PBS special on cartoonists. Cassady answered Adams's questions and encouraged him to submit his work. Adams sent his cartoons to a few publications for their consideration and promptly received rejection letters. He said, "Discouraged, I put my art supplies in the closet and decided to forget about cartooning."[3] But a year and a half later, Adams received another letter from Cassady. The cartoonist egged Adams on and told him not to get discouraged. Cassady assured him that his work was very good. That provided the motivation Adams needed to try again.

HELPING HIMSELF

Adams had been using his affirmations process in a number of areas. After graduating from college, he wanted to receive an MBA from the University of California at Berkeley; however, he had not scored high enough on the entrance exam to be accepted. With his new system for positive thinking, he tried again: He visualized his goal of scoring in the ninety-fourth percentile, wrote the goal down fifteen times each day, and prepared for the GMAT with study guides and practice exams. When he received his results from the test, he could hardly believe his eyes. He had scored in the ninety-fourth percentile.[4] And in 1986, Adams graduated from the University of California at Berkeley with an MBA.

Now on his second try at submitting cartoons to various publications,

How to Talk Yourself Out of Success

- I can never remember his name.
- I just always seem to dip into my savings.
- I lost my train of thought.
- I can never say that right.
- You can't teach an old dog new tricks.
- You can't have your cake and eat it too.
- I know my limitations.
- I'm just this way.
- I'm losing my mind.
- That makes me sick.
- Just my luck.
- That's out of my price range. I can't afford it.
- I don't have enough time.
- The ones I like don't like me, and the ones who like me—well, there's always something wrong with them.
- That's too rich for my blood.
- If I had money, I'd just worry about losing it.
- I'm living proof of Murphy's Law.
- I'll never understand those types of things.
- Everything I eat goes straight to my waist.
- Nobody wants to pay me what I'm worth.
- I used to have so much energy.
- My metabolism is slowing down.
- If such and such happens, I'm going to be sooo mad.

he took the same success steps by writing out fifteen times each day, "I will become a syndicated cartoonist."[5] It was a huge goal for an unknown artist. Maybe one in ten thousand cartoonists actually gets published. But Adams knew what he wanted, and he went for it. He put together a polished presentation of his work and sent it to syndicators. Two years later, *Dilbert* was published. And now, almost twenty years later, it is still read by millions of people each day as they flip to the comics or business section of their newspapers.

What Is Self-Talk?

Self-talk is most simply defined as what you say or think to yourself, either silently or aloud. Silent self-talk is commonly referred to as your thoughts, but it's actually a silent conversation that you hold in the privacy of your own mind. You are thinking all the time, day and night. In fact, psychologists estimate that the average person has between twenty thousand and sixty thousand thoughts per day. Every thought either moves you toward your goals and the person you intend to become or moves you away. No thoughts are neutral. Every thought counts. Unfortunately, approximately 90 percent of the thoughts you have today are repeats from yesterday and the day before, which is why effecting permanent, positive improvement in your life tends to be such an uphill challenge. The human mind loves the status quo, and if not trained otherwise, it will feed you a constant repetition of old ideas. Those old thoughts, like an automatic pilot, will steer your life in the same direction it has always gone.

On page 133 are some common examples of what people speak out loud or say to themselves silently.

Pay attention to almost any conversation for about eight or ten minutes, and you'll hear the toxic talk—the whining, complaining, blaming, condemning, and justifying. You'll hear people passionately arguing in favor of their most cherished limitations, and you'll also hear them knocking, sometimes subtly, those who have overcome those same limitations and done far more with their lives. Some insist that they're not being negative, just realistic; they're giving you an honest description of how their lives are right now. **The reality is that where you've been and what you've done matter far less than where you're going.** But if you persist in thinking and talking about current or prior performance, then where you've been, where you are, and where you're going will all be one and the same. This holds true for your golf game, your career, your marriage, and all the other areas of your life.

As King Solomon put it several thousand years ago, "As [a man] thinks in his heart, so is he" *(Proverbs 23:7, NKJV).*

BECOME A VISIONARY

The purpose of this lesson is to help you become a visionary with your life—someone who can sense things as they could be rather than just as they are, someone who acknowledges the sun when only clouds are visible. This is a vital skill in short supply, and when you master it, you can create opportunities for yourself and for others that most people won't even accept as a possibility.

Consider some part of your life that you'd like to improve. It could be a personal quality, a habit, an attitude, a financial problem, a challenge with your weight, or any other area of dissatisfaction. Since this area is below your standards, imagine yourself to be down in a hole, far beneath your potential. It doesn't matter so much how you got in the hole—just that you're aware that you're in the hole. To get out, you're going to have to think up, look up, speak up, and ultimately climb up. **Remember this as the first rule of holes: If you're in one, stop digging.** Most people have difficulty climbing out of the holes in their lives simply because they focus more on the hole (which represents their current circumstance) than on where they want to climb (which is the goal or solution). They are bogged down in the reality of today, and as a result, they'll keep getting more of what they already have.

You must make the shift from reactive thinking to proactive thinking. You must stop working for your mind and instead enlist your mind to work for you. Remember, your self-talk tends to work against you unless you are aware of it and use it to further your mission, goals, and ambitions.

For the rest of this lesson, I will use the word self-talk to refer to positive self-talk. **Positive self-talk involves thoughts you intentionally choose to think because of the results they will produce in your life.** It is a positive, assertive, present-tense description of a goal or other desired condition. It describes your character and lifestyle as it will be when you have fulfilled your potential and achieved your goals.

We all have ingrained beliefs about ourselves and our capabilities. A belief is a collection of subconscious thoughts that represent what you consider to be the absolute truth about any given situation in your life. Beliefs provide a feeling of absolute certainty. Your beliefs are literally hardwired, primarily through repetition, into neural pathways in your brain. Incoming data from your senses travels along these pathways on its way to interpretation in the brain. This means that prior to the brain's interpretation, incoming data is filtered through your beliefs. Reality is, therefore, not fixed but is manipulated by our beliefs. Self-talk represents specific mental energy that is received by the brain, then downloaded into neurological tracks and processed to create the actions we take.

We are not consciously aware of most of our beliefs because we have been living with them for so long. As a result, beliefs are like assumed truths that need not be questioned. And if we never challenge a belief, it sticks with us forever, becoming an ever-stronger conviction.

Typically, people will do just about anything to keep a belief intact, even if it is damaging or self-defeating. Since replacing a limiting or erroneous belief requires a combination of curiosity, humility, and courage, it's a rare occurrence. Many limiting beliefs also exonerate us from taking action and pursuing opportunities, from leaving our comfort zone or taking on greater responsibility. Still other limiting beliefs provide us with convenient alibis for doing less work.

WHAT IS REALITY?

It's important to remember that what we perceive as reality is not necessarily true at all, but only our personal version of reality. **We get only an edited look at the world around us.** This is because our beliefs, for better or for worse, act as filters, screening out any evidence that doesn't

How We Cling to Limiting Beliefs

1 | *We make life choices that harmonize with our beliefs.* We unconsciously choose situations and people that fit our preconceptions, while we avoid those people and situations that might weaken or contradict our beliefs. Our emotions, body language, and facial expressions also attract situations that match up with our beliefs.

2 | *We practice selective attention or inattention* depending on the circumstance. Our minds tune in to phenomena that confirm our beliefs while avoiding, ignoring, or deleting anything that could weaken the belief. We selectively remember events that fit our beliefs and selectively forget those that do not.

3 | *We automatically distort, mold, or exaggerate evidence* to reasonably fit our beliefs.

4 | As a last-ditch effort, *we may also rationalize contradictory evidence* to uphold a belief. Often this involves misinterpreting someone's motives or claiming an ulterior motive.

support them. We screen reality through our senses, our language, our inborn tendencies, and especially through generalizations we make relative to our personal experiences. It is in this fourth category of screening where we can make a substantial impact with positive self-talk. The beliefs that make up your self-concept come from the generalizations, many of them self-defeating, you have made throughout your life. In a number of different ways, we tend to cling to our limiting beliefs, like a child clings to a security blanket, even when there is evidence to the contrary.

The reason our unconscious goes to so much trouble to maintain our beliefs is that human beings have a subconscious tendency to continue doing what they've always done, to remain consistent with what they've said and done in the past. Any attempt to change current habits of thought or action triggers the homeostatic impulse, which makes you feel uneasy and uncomfortable. Since the human brain seeks comfort and pleasure and tries to avoid and move away from discomfort and pain, your natural tendency will be to go back to the old ways of doing things. While this tendency is common, it must be overcome if you are to come alive and unlock your full potential. You must be willing to be uncomfortable or uneasy if you want the rewards of higher levels of personal effectiveness.

The Mental Principles

To fully benefit from self-talk, you should understand the seven mental principles that support it. Principles by definition are timeless. They are in effect for everyone, everywhere, twenty-four hours a day. Just as physical laws do not discriminate, neither do the following mental laws:

1. Cause and effect. For every single effect in your life, there is a cause or group of causes. If you want to produce a specific result in your life, you must trace back from that result and identify the cause. The most important application of this principle is that your thoughts are causes and your circumstances are effects. In other words, causation is mental. Nothing happens by accident. Just because a cause cannot be determined does not mean there is no cause. However, many people attribute the effects in their lives—the results they achieve—to either good or bad luck. They do this for one of three reasons: (1) if it's bad luck, to relieve themselves of a sense of responsibility, which deflects attention from the true source; (2) if it's good luck, to appear modest or humble; or (3) because they are ignorant of the true cause.

 Successful men and women train their minds to think only about what they want to happen in their lives.

2. Belief. The principle of belief says that whatever you believe about yourself long enough and deeply enough becomes true for you. According to your beliefs is it done unto you. Whatever you tell yourself repeatedly with feeling, you eventually come to believe. You do not believe what you see so much as you see what you have already decided to believe. For the most part, **your beliefs produce your life experiences, not the other way around.** Throughout childhood, you developed beliefs as a result of your most dominant exposures. For example, you learned beliefs from your parents, teachers, friends, and the media, as well as from your own interpretations of your life experiences. As you've moved through life, but especially during childhood, you've acquired a host of beliefs that are either partially or completely false. Many such limiting beliefs are in direct contradiction to what the Bible says is possible for you. And, once a belief is locked in, you tend to notice only those things that reinforce that your belief is true. This selective perception allows you to experience your own personal version of reality.

3. Subconscious activity. Any emotionally charged thought or idea that is repeatedly held in your conscious mind is interpreted by your subconscious mind as a command. You hold a thought in your mind when you dwell on it, mull it over, and consistently talk about it. Since the subconscious mind cannot distinguish between truth and fantasy, it accepts verbal input without regard to present reality. In effect, the subconscious is a perfect servant. It always agrees with and complies with what the conscious mind tells it. It becomes like a parrot, repeating and replaying the commands you've given it. **Your job is to convince the subconscious that the condition you desire already exists.** Once you do that, your subconscious then arouses your awareness to the opportunities around you that are consistent with your goals. You will attract into your life the ideas, events, and circumstances that harmonize with your most dominant self-talk.

4. Substitution. The conscious mind can hold only one thought at a time, either positive or negative. This means you are always free to choose a better thought than your current thought. Ask yourself, "How's my thinking been working—in my marriage, my career, my faith, my health, and so forth?" If your current thinking is not leading to the results you desire, it is up to you to change your thoughts. But be aware that you cannot eliminate a thought directly. You can do so only by substituting another one for it. If I say to you, "Don't think of an orange elephant," you, of course, immediately think of it. If you say, "I refuse to think of an orange elephant," then you're still thinking about it. If someone tells you not to worry, you will continue to worry because you can't concentrate on the reverse of something. It's not possible. But if I give you something else specific to think about, then the new thought displaces the current thought. You can get rid of that orange elephant by thinking of a big white horse. This is the principle of substitution. Thoughts of worry are replaced with thoughts of faith and confidence. Thoughts of boldness replace thoughts of fear. You can exert control over your thinking and, by extension, your life by replacing any negative, counterproductive thoughts with positive, empowering thoughts.

> Whatever you direct your mind to think about will ultimately be revealed for everyone to see.

5. Mental equivalency. This principle states that before physical creation, there must first be mental creation. Just as an artist must have a vision of what she is painting before her brush touches the canvas, you too must clearly see the end result of what you are striving to create in your life. Improvement in your circumstances is always preceded by improvement in your mental pictures, by improvement in the dominant images that occupy your mind. This means that **you must develop a**

7 Mental Principles

1 | Cause and Effect

2 | Belief

3 | Subconscious Activity

4 | Substitution

5 | Mental Equivalency

6 | Concentration

7 | Relaxation

vivid mental picture of any goal you hope to achieve in advance of its actual accomplishment. Before you can have something new and different in your life, before you can have something new and different on the outside, you must become new and different on the inside, or in the way you think. An architect must cultivate the mental version of the home he is designing before he develops the actual blueprint. Responsible parents must envision their children today as the successful adults they intend for them to become. A place kicker must first kick a forty-five-yard field goal in his head before he actually kicks it with his foot. You must be willing to let go of the old you to make room for the new you. You must be willing to shake yourself free of your old pictures, of your old ways of thinking and doing, if you truly desire a new and improved life experience. Positive self-talk strengthens your upgraded mental equivalent, causing it to become a powerful magnetic force, attracting into your life exactly what you need to reach your goals.

6. Concentration. The principle of concentration states that whatever you focus on grows and expands. You will be effective to the degree that you can concentrate single-mindedly on only one thing and stick with it until it's complete. If you dwell on your positive experiences, your blessings, your goals, and all the people who love you, then you will attract even more blessings, even more love, and even more accomplishments. The more you emphasize your good health, the healthier you feel. The more you dwell on your spouse's positive qualities, the stronger your relationship will become. This works for good or for bad, so be careful where you place your mental priorities. Whatever you stop thinking about or turn your attention away from tends to fall out of your life. So refuse to entertain thoughts of doubt, fear, or worry. See if you can go twenty-four hours with thoughts only of joy, abundance, praise, and optimism. See if you can go an entire day without a hint of fear, criticism, or negativity of any kind in your thoughts and conversations.

The apostle Paul describes this principle in Philippians 4:8: "Fix your thoughts on what is true, and honorable, and right, and pure, and lovely, and admirable. Think about things that are excellent and worthy of praise" (NLT).

You can build any virtue into your mentality by dwelling on that virtue every single day. So choose to think about good things! For more insights into this maxim and for specific strategies on increasing your joy quotient, I encourage you to pick up a copy of my book *The 4:8 Principle*.

7. Relaxation. Trying too hard mentally actually becomes counterproductive. Too much mental effort eventually tends to defeat itself. With a physical task, the harder you work, the faster you progress. The harder you work at digging a hole in the ground, the sooner you'll have a ditch. The harder you hammer a nail, the faster it penetrates a two-by-four. But when you try to force things mentally—or press, as it is referred to by athletes—your mind freezes up and stops working creatively. This generally produces more of what you don't want. Your subconscious absorbs positive self-talk fastest when you are relaxed and unhurried. Thoughts of worry, fear, anxiety, and doubt are all signs of a mental tug-of-war that must be eliminated. But wrestling with an unwanted thought just injects it with more power. Instead, calmly and gently replace it with a positive or constructive idea, and the negative thought will fade away. Practice blending your self-talk with a calm sense of positive expectancy, the feeling and knowing that God is in control of everything. As Romans 8:28 says, "We know that in all things God works for the good of those who love him, who have been called according to his purpose" (NIV). **Remember that God is always committed to your well-being.**

The P.E.P.P. Formula

Effective self-talk is created by using the P.E.P.P. formula: positively phrased, emotion provoking, present tense, and personal.

Use specific, precise, *positively phrased* language in your self-talk. Say, "I am reading for one hour every evening" rather than, "I am no longer wasting my evenings watching TV." Instead of affirming, "I am not eating ice cream," say, "I am eating only nutrient-dense, high-energy foods." Since your mind thinks in pictures, it has trouble processing a negatively stated goal. It's difficult, if not impossible, for your mind to create a picture of yourself *not* doing something. Stating self-talk positively also shifts your awareness from what you don't want to what you do want.

Next, your self-talk should be *emotion provoking,* causing you to feel some of the emotions even before the experience. The more feeling you intermingle with your self-talk, the more quickly it impacts the subconscious. Experiment with using bold words that are fun and passionate. Use words you haven't used much before. Break the verbal rut. Also, try adding feeling words such as *easily, joyfully, radically, effortlessly, boldly, infinitely,* or *gratefully* into your self-talk statements.

Next, your self-talk should always be in the *present tense.* The subconscious mind, where permanent change becomes rooted, does not recognize the past or the future. It operates only in the here and now. You can effect subconscious change best by communicating in the language your subconscious mind understands: the present tense. The theory of cognitive dissonance states that when you hold two psychologically inconsistent thoughts, you experience dissonance, or a sense of tension and inharmonious feelings. The subconscious, in an attempt to reduce the discomfort of the conflicting messages, does everything it can to create the most recently imposed suggestion or self-talk. **Repetition of a specific self-talk statement narrows the gap between conflicting conscious and subconscious beliefs.** With persistent repetition, old neurological grooves are erased and replaced, in effect creating upgraded mental software. Your subconscious computer then supplies you with the words, actions, instincts, mannerisms, body language, creativity, emotions, and other responses consistent with the most dominant mental images imprinted on the brain.

Initially, using present tense can feel a bit uncomfortable because you are speaking about the future as if it's already here. Since this is not the way most of us learned to communicate, it's bound to feel strange. Just accept that this is how your mind works. When you affirm your goals and dreams as if they're already attained, you make the shift from being bogged down to being a visionary. **The most powerful words in the English language are those that come after the words *I am.***

The last *P* is for *personal.* Self-talk that you design yourself—that is

Positively phrased

Emotion provoking

Present tense

Personal

personal to your circumstances, your character, and your goals—is most effective. You'll experience the strongest connection to the self-talk you have composed yourself. However, when you begin, it's often helpful to borrow self-talk from other sources, and then edit to personalize it. **Any self-talk repeated often enough will be internalized and become part of your unique mental makeup.**

Formulating Your Own Self-Talk*

Because everything you think or say should lead to the fulfillment of your purpose and the accomplishment of your goals, you must regularly review your personal mission statement and identify your most important life goals. In addition, you should be clear why those goals are important to you and how you are going to accomplish them—the action plan! So before attempting to create your own self-talk, invest the time and mental effort, as discussed in lessons 2 and 3, to clarify the what, the why, and the how. After you have determined the results you're striving for, imagine you have already achieved those results. See

*To request a FREE set of sample positive affirmations, please visit
   www.1percentclub.com/selftalk.

yourself as already in possession of your most important goals. Think "as if," and experience the satisfaction and sense of accomplishment. Now ask yourself this key question: "If I had already accomplished these goals, what would I believe about myself that I don't now truly believe?" Make a list of what comes to your mind. What would you believe about yourself, your abilities, your mental resilience, your personal habits, and your potential? What would you believe about your lifestyle? What would you believe about your finances in particular or the economy in general? What would you believe about the world? Finally, what would you believe about your particular future?

Answering these questions is a proactive way to develop the mind-set of the person you must become if you want to reach your goals. Before you can have, you must do; but before you can do, you must first become. And if you don't lay the foundation of becoming the right person, then whatever you achieve will certainly slip away. It will not—in fact, it cannot—be permanent.

Let me share another technique for clarifying your beliefs: Think of one of the most compelling goals you want to achieve in the next three years. Develop a clear picture of it in your mind. Now answer this simple but profound question: Why don't you have it already? If your goal is to be financially independent and that's very important to you, then why aren't you already financially independent? Why haven't you already accomplished this goal? Whatever answers you come up with, whether they are logical, factual, or mathematical, and whether they are exaggerations, distortions, fears, or other excuses of the imagination, they are still real as far as accomplishing your goal is concerned. Every answer you come up with represents a limited belief or a blind spot in your mental equivalent. Self-talk helps you shore up your mental equivalent. It gives you the ability to create and fortify beliefs that support the person you want to become and the goals you want to achieve.

You can turn any of your answers to your advantage by practicing *positive opposite therapy,* which activates the principle of substitution.

Positive opposite therapy provides you with the mental nourishment that must come before achieving goals. If you dwell on positive beliefs

If becoming financially independent is your goal, then your answers to the question "Why haven't you already . . . ?" may sound something like this:

- I'm too young to be financially independent.
- I didn't start planning soon enough.
- I don't deserve it yet.
- I need to get into another field.
- I'm not up on good investment strategies.
- My goals weren't set high enough.
- I think it takes about thirty years to get rich.
- I still waste too much time on paperwork.
- I've got too many family expenses right now.
- Taxes are too high.
- Interest rates are too low.
- And so on . . .

about yourself, they will take root and multiply into strong convictions, which will override old negative beliefs. You can best deploy your mental energies by focusing on where you want to go rather than where you are or where you've been. Remember, you can and do—either intentionally or haphazardly—determine what you believe. What you choose to believe about yourself is completely up to you. The important question is this: What should you believe? In light of who you intend to become during your lifetime, what must you believe today in order to achieve the right results tomorrow? We know that beliefs come first and results come second. So what should you believe? An accurate answer to this question requires that you first develop complete clarity about your future. The clearer your vision for the future is, the easier it will be to determine what you must first believe in order to get there.

THE PERSON YOU MUST BECOME

When formulating your self-talk, consider the things you will need in order to meet your goals: certain skills, habits, knowledge, and attitude; particular virtues; different qualities; and specific belief systems. Ask yourself, "What sort of person do I need to be before I can achieve these goals?"

Composing your own self-talk forces you to look at accomplishing your goals from all angles. Ask yourself, "What skills do I need to develop?" Then, when you've determined those skills, turn them into a self-talk statement. For example, to develop communication skills,

---

Simply create self-talk statements that are close to the opposite of the limiting belief. For example:

- *"I'm too young to become financially independent"* becomes "I am the perfect age to enjoy financial independence."

- *"I still waste too much time on paperwork"* becomes "I focus on new-business generation and delegate everything else."

- *"I don't deserve it yet"* becomes "I am ready for and worthy of financial independence right now."

constantly affirm, "I communicate effectively; I listen well, and I ask good questions." Do the same thing with habits. Determine the habits you need to develop—the things you need to do regularly to become the person you've described and to reach the goals you want to achieve—and then affirm that you already have that habit. Similarly, affirm that you already have the knowledge you need, and affirm that you already have the qualities, characteristics, virtues, and attitudes in place. Think as if you're already the person you want to become.

As you are formulating your self-talk statements, try to use the word *now* either at the beginning or near the end: "I am now achieving goals faster than ever before." "I accept myself completely right now." Also, experiment with using action words such as *doing, achieving, satisfying, winning, accumulating, creating, finding, helping, loving.* Using action words in your self-talk statements helps you to imagine yourself already in possession of the goal.

The majority of your self-talk statements should start with the word *I* or *my.* I have also found that adding one of the following phrases is particularly helpful in forming positive affirmations:

> expect . . .
> am ready for . . .
> am prepared . . .
> am open to . . .
> accept . . .
> receive . . .
> love . . .
> am comfortable with . . .
> allow . . .
> am worthy of . . .
> am willing . . .
> deserve . . .

Decide what you want to create in your life, and then plug these key words into your self-talk statements. Relentlessly repeat that you *expect* to reach your goal—that you're *ready* for it, *prepared* for it, *open* to it;

that you *accept* it into your life; that you now *receive* it; and that you're *comfortable* with it. Repeatedly affirm that you are *worthy* of your goal, that you *love* it, that you *deserve* it, and finally, that you are *willing* to do whatever it takes to reach it. The nature of these authoritative commands reduces the psychological resistance to change and helps prevent a retreat into your comfort zone. So bombard yourself with thoughts like these. Drive them into your mind so that they penetrate the subconscious. To receive a free set of self-talk cards to help you accelerate your progress, please visit www.successisnotanaccident.com.

STRENGTHEN YOUR MIND

Remember, much of life is simply an exercise in strengthening your mind. A flabby mind allows a continuous stream of thoughts swirling at a hundred miles per hour, never channeled in a single direction for any length of time. Your every thought or word triggers an image. Then, like a computer's operating instructions, those images act on you. So make the inner shift from taking commands to giving commands, to becoming a deliberate and purposeful thinker. Like anything else, with practice, winning self-talk will become a reflex. You'll begin to consistently amaze yourself and others.

SILENT TALK

There are several ways to use self-talk. The first is silent talk, or taking control of the thoughts that occupy your mind. Simply repeat specific self-talk statements to yourself over and over. Think what you want to think about. This serves several purposes: First, it keeps you focused on your goals—on what you desire versus what you fear. Second, silent talk trains your mind to think purposefully instead of randomly. You become a proactive thinker rather than a reactive thinker. These silent conversations then gradually become your habitual thinking pattern. What began as a challenging attempt to improve your thinking becomes an effortless and highly productive mental habit. The third benefit of silent talk is that it interrupts and blocks out stale, self-defeating thinking through the principle of substitution.

VERBALIZATION

Verbalization, or audible self-talk, serves the same purpose as silent talk but is considerably more persuasive and powerful. Anything you say aloud with passion and conviction has twice the impact of what you say quietly to yourself. This is because you're involving more of your brain by using more of your senses. The more senses you involve, the faster

 Many people say things to themselves that they would never, ever say to a respected friend. Be a respected friend to yourself. Be a nourishing friend to yourself.

your self-talk is internalized and absorbed by your subconscious. And the faster you internalize the instructions, the faster you improve. By hearing yourself speak the thought, you complete what psycholinguists call the language loop. This creates a double reinforcement because your ears hear your voice giving the order. So repeat your self-talk like you really mean it. Go for volume, if that stirs up more sensation; shout your self-talk. **Remember, you are in charge of delivering operating instructions to your subconscious. If you don't do it, someone else will. You can count on it.** Do what you have to do to get the message across. The most important person for you to impress is yourself. And if you convince yourself, you can convince the world.

If you're just getting started with audible self-talk, you may want to experiment with it privately at first. If you drive solo to work in the morning, you have a wonderful opportunity to shout your self-talk aloud. You'll get your day off to a powerful start and avoid the venom of most morning radio shows. You might even break the monotony of the morning commute and bring a smile to the face of other drivers who spot you chatting with yourself. Verbalizing in the shower is another easy way to prepare for a fantastic day. Even sing your self-talk. Just make up songs that affirm the reality you want to create. Everybody has a good voice in the shower.

MIRROR TALK

If you are willing to feel a little uncomfortable at first, you will find that mirror talk generates an intense emotional reaction. The way to do it is this: Choose one specific self-talk command to practice. Then go stand confidently and erect in front of a mirror, preferably a full-length mirror, and make good eye contact with yourself. It's been said that the eyes are the window to the soul, and after you try this method, you'll realize just what that means. Look deeply into your eyes and repeat your self-talk aloud, with as much feeling as possible. Recite your single, specific command fifty to one hundred times, and resist the urge to break eye contact.

This technique often produces an invigorating emotional reaction, particularly when the self-talk concerns your self-esteem and self-worth. However, many people find that a surge of subconscious negativity rises to the surface. This is okay—in fact, it's vitally important, because uncovering limiting and destructive beliefs is the first step to eliminating them. If you doubt the effectiveness of this method, try it just before you go to sleep, affirming with enthusiasm, "I am alert with boundless energy! I am alert with boundless energy!" while looking into your eyes in front of a mirror. Then see if you can drift right to sleep. You'll quickly become a believer!

PARTNER TALK

In partner talk, you provide your spouse or a trusted friend with a set of self-talk statements phrased in the second person. For example, your partner might affirm to you: "You are lean, muscular, and confident. You believe in yourself. You earn $100,000 in annual income." Your partner speaks affirmations to you, and you accept each affirmation by responding, "Yes, I am" or "Yes, I do, thank you." Then switch roles and do the same for your partner. Remember, what other people say to you strongly influences your self-image. Permanent improvement on the outside comes only after you improve your self-image. And when used intentionally, suggestions from others can powerfully override old scripts and reinforce new, positive habits of thought and behavior.

A more casual variation of this method is to make an agreement with a friend or your spouse that each time you see or speak to each other, he or she will affirm that you already have a particular quality or have already accomplished a specific goal. Since your subconscious mind processes

Silent Talk

Verbalization

Question
Suggestion

Mirror Talk

Self-Talk

Self-Script

Partner Talk

Written Self-Talk

Self-Conversation

positive assertive statements about you from others as if they were fact, there is no limit to the progress you can make. Repeated suggestions from others tend to carry a lot of weight. In The 1% Club, we greet one another with a genuine "congratulations" instead of the conventional "hello."

SELF-CONVERSATION

Self-conversation is an advanced form of subconscious programming that requires people to hold down both ends of a dialogue. Self-conversation works well because it most closely resembles the continuous, unconscious inner dialogue we have with ourselves. This typically consists of repeated question-and-answer sessions that are often stimulated by our environmental exposures and circumstances. In other words, our inner dialogue tends to be a random, reactive dialogue rather than a purposeful one. The question-answer format is our brain's way of evaluating our experiences.

To practice self-conversation, write down a series of important questions concerning your character and your goals, along with the corresponding answers to each of the questions. The aim of this exercise is to crystallize the most perfect response to each of the questions. How would you like to be able to answer each one? An easy way to organize your self-conversation is to use note cards. Take six to ten note cards and write a question on one side and the answer on the other. Read the questions and corresponding answers several times a day, either silently or aloud. Repeated use of this technique trains your mind to entertain only empowering inner dialogues—conversations that lead you in positive directions. You get in the habit of asking better questions and giving better answers. You control the inner dialogue rather than it controlling you.

Here's one example of a question: "Good morning. How are you doing today?" The answer you write is up to you, but it might go something like this: "I'm terrific this morning. I got just the right amount of sleep, and I'm raring to go. I'm clear about my goals and what I must do to reach them. I expect the best of myself and others today, and that's exactly what I'm going to get."

Your note cards should include a mix of specific goal-related questions along with general attitude- or character-type questions. The answers you give are really just self-talk in response to a particular question. This method works because the question tends to make your subconscious more receptive to the answer. It conditions the soil, so to speak. This method is fun and effective if you can move beyond the initial feelings of silliness or embarrassment. You'll rapidly begin to notice a subtle change in your outlook,

 Whatever you emphasize consciously gets impressed subconsciously.

habits, and what you say when you talk to yourself. For extra effect, have your spouse or accountability partner ask you one or more questions from your note cards.

WRITTEN SELF-TALK

Written self-talk is the consistent practice of writing and rewriting your goals and supportive self-talk statements. Rewriting your self-talk is a psychoneural muscular activity that helps align your subconscious beliefs with your conscious goals. Each time you rewrite your self-talk, it becomes clearer and more real. Writing involves thinking of a desired outcome, printing it on paper, and then reviewing it when finished. It forces you to integrate several senses toward the same result, which helps you internalize the self-talk. Your written, present-tense description activates your reticular cortex, the portion of your brain that determines what you are aware of. **Each time you rewrite your self-talk, you become increasingly more alert to the wisdom, ideas, information, people, and other resources that can help you achieve your goals.** Rewriting five to ten of these thoughts or affirmations on a regular basis causes your mind to interpret them as having much more significance than your other twenty thousand to sixty thousand thoughts per day. As a result, your awareness concerning those self-talk commands will be heightened. You become hypersensitive to what moves you toward your goal and what does not. Whatever you emphasize consciously gets impressed subconsciously. **Whatever you *express* becomes *impressed*.**

Since you think in pictures, be sure to print your self-talk in bold block letters. This gives your brain a distinct image to absorb. It also takes longer to print, forcing you to be still, concentrate, and think more deeply about the person you want to become and the goals you intend to achieve. Simultaneously writing and reading your self-talk affects you at a very deep level—like a double shot of energy but without caffeine.

Written self-talk is effective anytime, but especially first thing in the morning and right before you go to sleep. During these two periods (within approximately fifteen minutes after waking and fifteen minutes prior to falling asleep), your brain-wave activity slows down and puts you in a highly suggestive or programmable state. Written self-talk channels your attention toward what's most important and away from what's least important. It doesn't have to take any more than four to eight minutes, and you will find it's an inspiring and refreshing way to start and end each day. Feel free to revise your self-talk as you go if you think of better ways to express it.

Rewriting your goals on a regular basis may also help you uncover any conflicting beliefs you have about a particular goal. Constantly rewriting your goals tends to become a positive addiction if your goals are right for you. On the other hand, if a goal is not right for you, you may develop an aversion to constantly rewriting it, almost like a body rejects an incompatible organ. This is a valuable clue that you might be on the wrong path, and it may save you months or even years of frustrated effort.

SELF-SCRIPT

Self-script involves recording your personal self-talk onto an audio recorder. Listening to yourself repeatedly give positive commands is an easy way to reprogram yourself. To make your own self-script, choose ten to twelve positively phrased statements that support your goals. Remember the P.E.P.P. formula: Make your self-script positive, emotion provoking, present tense, and personal. You can concentrate on one area of life for all the statements, or you can divide them among different areas. I prefer to specialize by concentrating on one area per recording or at least per track. Once you've decided on the self-talk statements, you'll need a digital recorder and a CD player to provide background music.

Classical music tends to work best, helping you to relax and absorb as you listen, but any type of relaxing instrumental music will do. Read your self-talk into the recorder as the music plays in the background. Repeat each of your statements three to five times before moving to the next one. Also, it's a good idea to alternate between a strong and commanding voice, a relaxed statement, and a whisper.

The first round of self-talk should always contain present-tense, first-person statements. Keep repeating the cycle of self-talk to the end of the recording. You may also want to repeat the cycle in the second person as if someone else is affirming you. For example: "You are goal directed." Listen to your new script as often as possible. Remember, it's not important that you always pay close attention. If you can hear it, you will be gaining a benefit. You may also want to record a present-tense description of your ideal day, your personal mission statement, or any important upcoming event you'll be involved in.

QUESTION SUGGESTION

The last self-talk method is what I call question suggestion, an indirect and subtle technique for programming your subconscious mind. Question suggestion is the deliberate process of asking yourself specific questions that presuppose the conditions and circumstances you desire. To help you better understand, let me first give you some common examples of negative suggestive questions:

Why can't I ever lose that last five pounds?

Why am I always so tired when I wake up?

How come I keep getting distracted?

How did I get to be so klutzy?

Why do I always dip into my savings?

Why am I never given the credit I deserve?

Why do I always sell myself short?

What makes the above questions negative and self-limiting is that they are structured in a way that actually assumes, or takes for granted, the unwanted condition. If you ask, "How did I get to be so klutzy?" you're first of all assuming that you are, in fact, a klutz rather than just somebody who in the past has occasionally acted klutzy. Second, you're commanding your subconscious to manufacture evidence that supports your assumption. In other words, you are setting in motion a disappointing self-fulfilling prophecy. Remember, your subconscious obediently complies with the directives you or others give it. Watch out for the presumptive questions of those you live and work with. Are their questions helping or hurting you?

Bring Out the Best
Question suggestion helps you take conscious control of the questions you repeatedly ask yourself. Your thinking can be only as good as the questions you ask, so ask those that direct your attention to the best things in your life. Ask questions that challenge your creativity and potential. Ask possibility questions. Ask questions that bring out the best in you. Here are some examples:

Aren't I fortunate to be so healthy?

Aren't I fortunate to have tons of energy?

How can I be even more productive today and enjoy the process?

What might happen this week that would bring me total pleasure and satisfaction?

I wonder how many lives I will positively impact today?

Isn't it great that I'm always in the right place at the right time?

The above questions are empowering because they assume a positive, desired condition or outcome. When I ask, "Aren't I fortunate to be so healthy?" the suggestion is, "I am already very healthy." That's how the brain interprets it. When I ask, "Isn't it great that I'm always in the right place at the right time?" I am really programming myself to be in the right place at the right time. When I ask, "Aren't I fortunate to have tons of energy?" I am affirming that I already have a lot of energy.

You'll find that questions immediately change what you're focusing on and consequently change your feelings and your level of creativity, excitement, and motivation.

Aren't you fortunate to be reading this lesson?

Fifteen Practical Insights

Here are fifteen key ideas or insights that will help you talk yourself into even more success and get the most out of this lesson.

1 | Always use the word *when* rather than *if* in situations where you are talking about something you want to happen. Say, "When I close that sale" or "When I lose that weight . . ."

2 | Take control of your explanatory style—that is, the way you interpret past events. Put a positive twist on things—or spin them to your benefit, as they say in politics—by looking back and reinterpreting any seemingly negative situation and mentally downplaying its significance. This reduces the effect the past has on your future.

3 | Watch out for media programming, the constant suggestive influence from radio, television, newspaper, magazines, and billboards. It is estimated that the average American is exposed to more than fifteen hundred advertising messages each day. If you think like the masses think, you'll get what the masses get. Let's not go there.

4 | Never let anyone say anything to you or about you in your presence that you don't sincerely want to happen. Be alert whenever someone starts a sentence with the word *you* in daily conversations. Your interactions with others play a major role in what you believe to be true about yourself. Sometimes it's minor. Sometimes it's major. But everything counts! Be especially cognizant of old friends who continue to speak of you as the person you used to be but no longer want to be. Though you can't control what others say to you, you can increase the amount of time you invest with people who are positive and encouraging. For close friends and family, be bold and ask them to verbally support your efforts to grow and improve.

5 | In dealing with other people, particularly those you live or work with, never characterize them in their presence as something you don't want them to be. You will just reinforce their tendency to be that way. If you want people to be on time more often, the very worst thing you can do is to shout at them or look them in the eye and say, "You're always late!" Avoid this temptation, or you'll keep getting more of the same.

6 | Whenever you catch yourself thinking something negative or self-defeating, say the word *cancel, next,* or *deflect*. Then say or think what you really want to believe. This technique interrupts and weakens limiting patterns of thought.

7 | By always doing what you say, you strengthen your character and literally program yourself to create the reality dictated by your words. So resolve to keep every single agreement you make with yourself, and your

self-talk will become even more powerful. In other words, walk your talk.

8 | Refuse to claim or take possession of anything that you don't want in your lifestyle. For example, don't say "my cold," "my headache," "my bad back," "my debt," or "my price range." Instead, attach yourself mentally and verbally to what you *do* want, such as peace of mind, joy, strong relationships, abundance, and good health.

9 | No matter how common it may be, refuse to get cornered into conversations involving skepticism, cynicism, doubt, fear, worry, or gossip. Self-talk is contagious. Don't let others contaminate your self-talk with their negativity and toxic energy. Talk to yourself and others only about things you want to experience.

10 | Most people routinely say things to or about themselves that they would never say to a respected friend. Refuse to acknowledge any thoughts that oppose who you really want to be. Make this promise: Be a respected and nourishing friend to yourself!

11 | Leave the past in the past. If it becomes necessary to discuss a habit, tendency, or quality that you'd rather not have, always talk about it as if it's long gone—as if it's history rather than a current, ongoing problem. Use the phrases "up until now," "in the past," or "I used to be" to frame any constructive self-criticism. Be careful not to pull the past into the future by making generalizations about prior behavior.

12 | Choose the words of champions. Replace "I'll try to" with "I will." Replace "I didn't have time" with "I chose

not to make time for that." Replace "It's not my fault" with "I accept responsibility." Replace "You make me upset" with "I feel upset when . . ." You always have the choice. You can be a helpless victim, or you can be a powerful human being who makes an impact on the world.

13 | Watch out for others who transplant their past experiences to you, often lowering your expectations and in effect causing you to clench up, preparing for the worst. This is particularly true concerning life's common experiences such as school exams, dating, marriage, pregnancy and childbirth, raising children, finances, and getting older. Learn from others' experience, but always assume it's going to be a lot better for you than it was for them. Remember, what you expect with confidence tends to materialize. So be alert to the sort of mass hypnotism that goes on in our society.

14 | Every cell in your body "listens in" to your thinking and interprets each thought as a command. If you want to know what your self-talk was like three years ago, just look at yourself and your life today. What the mind harbors, the body expresses.

15 | Putting into practice even just a few suggestions from this lesson will generate a visible and measurable improvement in your life. Don't worry about mistakes. Shrug them off and stay focused on doing better tomorrow. Remember, it is at the very moment that you think your self-talk is not working that you need to use it the most. Fill up every spare moment with a thought of the person you want to be.

You Are Changing!

Finally, remember this: At this very moment, you are changing! Nobody stays the same for any length of time. You are continually changing in the specific direction that your thoughts and goals lead you. You are *what* you are and *where* you are because of the dominating thoughts you have allowed to occupy your mind. Your surroundings are nothing more than the outworking of your thoughts. There is only one thing in the world that you have complete control over, and that is your thinking. If you don't deliberately give yourself positive directions, your mind and your body will continue to act upon directions from anywhere and everywhere, like a vacuum sucking up dirt. There's no real argument on this point. It's easier to do nothing and just take life as it comes to you. But you have a choice: You can be programmed by your fears and doubts, by envious peers and fair-weather friends, by the flood of bad news and negative headlines—or you can chart your own course and let others follow. It's completely up to you.

Do you now have the intensity of purpose, the tenacity, to discipline your mind to stay fixed on what you want? If you do, your mind will become transformed with confidence and boldness. Using the tool of positive self-talk, you can eliminate negative thought patterns and replace them with positive beliefs and expectations. Using self-talk, you can make the internal adjustments that must precede all external changes. You can get much more out of life than most people ever look for. You are mentally tough! And I know you can do it!

Lesson 5 Questions for Reflection

Which of your beliefs about yourself are not useful and could be limiting your full potential?

In light of who you intend to become, how should you improve your self-talk?

What captures your attention immediately before falling asleep at night and upon awakening in the morning?

What do you tend to think about most when you are not thinking about your goals?

What does the Bible teach regarding the pitfalls of an undisciplined mind? Consider Proverbs 4:23, 27:19; Matthew 12:36-37; Romans 12:2; 2 Corinthians 10:5; Philippians 4:8; James 1:8.

Whom can you influence with the ideas from this lesson in the next forty-eight hours?

LESSON 5 ASSIGNMENTS

1 | Make a list of what you would believe about your-self, your potential, and the world if you had already achieved your most important goal.

2 | On separate note cards, neatly write at least ten self-talk statements (affirmations) for each of your top five three-year goals.

3 | Read aloud the Fifteen Practical Insights on pages 159–162.

LESSON 6

Choose
Positive Visualization

Positive results follow positive mental pictures.

In this lesson, you will learn to

- Discipline your mind

- Sharpen your concentration ability

- Reinforce commitment to goals

- Increase desire

- Build productive beliefs

- Reduce stress

- Accelerate your progress

A subconscious programming technique even more powerful than positive self-talk is *positive visualization*—mentally picturing events or outcomes in your mind before they occur in physical reality. Visualization is based on the same principles as self-talk, but it is considerably more effective because it goes directly to the source: the collection of subconscious mental pictures that occupy your mind. Self-talk triggers the development of new mental images, whereas visualization directly imprints the new pictures. Self-talk and visualization complement each other. Visualization intensifies your self-talk, and self-talk reinforces your visualization. Both techniques promote the accomplishment of your goals and should be used in tandem on a consistent basis.

It's important to note that visualization is a skill that can be learned and mastered. Everyone has the ability to visualize. As with all other skills, some people find visualization naturally easier, almost intuitive, while others must practice often to experience the benefits. You can demonstrate your ability to visualize just by thinking of how many

> I visualized where I wanted to be, what kind of player I wanted to become. I knew exactly where I wanted to go, and I focused on getting there.
> —*Michael Jordan*

windows there are in your living room or recalling the smell of freshly baked chocolate-chip cookies. Visualization refers not just to visual images but also to hearing, touch, taste, smell, and emotional sensations.

It has been said that the pictures you create in your head turn into the reality you hold in your hand. That's why it is crucial that you not allow the visualization process to be arbitrary. The primary aim of this lesson is to help you make the shift from random, reactive visualizations to deliberate, proactive visualizations that support who you want to become and what you want to accomplish.

For the rest of this lesson, I will teach you exactly what visualization means and how it works. We'll discuss variations of visualization as well as how to enhance your visualization skills to help you maximize your performance in every area of life.

Your subconscious mind is responsible for your long-term success,

failure, or mediocrity. It is responsible for generating and coordinating your thoughts, feelings, words, and actions. This is good news because *you* are responsible for the subconscious mind and whether it is programmed for success. Once again, you are in charge. You have yet another opportunity to take control of the direction of your life *if*—and this is a big *if*—you are willing to be extraordinarily picky about which thoughts occupy your mind. While you cannot always control what you are exposed to and the thoughts these exposures stimulate, you can control what you choose to dwell upon. The thoughts you harbor most often impact your life the most. The thoughts that set up camp in your mind have the most influence, not those that merely drop in for a quick visit.

Fortunately, your subconscious mind is not a master, but an ever-ready and willing servant. It will bring into your life whatever you sincerely ask. The subconscious is not discriminating. **Like fertile soil, your subconscious will accommodate whatever seeds you choose to plant.** It's just as happy to help you as to hurt you. It is content to bring you health or sickness and fatigue. It is happy to bring you either abundance or lack. Your mind works on the instructions it is given. These instructions can come from its owner—you—or they can come from whatever influences you expose yourself to on a regular basis. It is up to you to give your subconscious mind instructions that will produce a life that will make you contagiously happy and fully alive.

An instruction to your subconscious can be defined as any continuously held conscious thought. It is not the infrequent mental pictures that exert tremendous influence, but the most dominant ones. **The images that you consciously and repeatedly focus on become absorbed into the subconscious mind, like water into a sponge.** At this point the progress is made or the damage is done.

Successful men and women train their minds to think about what they want to have happen in their lives. They think about the type of person they want to become. They think about their goals and dreams. They think about the principles and virtues they most admire. They think about the people they like and the situations they hope to experience. By contrast, the unsuccessful or mediocre lack mental discipline.

What If?

What if you visualized (one hundred times) pushing away a dessert after taking only one bite. Do you think you'd be more likely to do that in real circumstances?

What if you visualized (one hundred times) delivering your next presentation comfortably and excellently. Do you think that would have a positive impact on your results?

What if you visualized (one hundred times) the physical condition you hope to be in when you turn sixty. Do you think that would have any effect on the lifestyle habits you choose today?

What if you visualized (one hundred times) rising easily and effortlessly at 5 a.m. feeling completely refreshed and rejuvenated. Do you believe that would improve your effectiveness in the morning?

Their thoughts drift from the circumstances they hope to avoid to the people they dislike and the wide variety of injustices that seem to surround them. They're quick to dismiss themselves as being unlucky and even quicker to dismiss the successful as being extremely lucky. The mediocre bathe themselves in all the reasons why they can't have the life they really want, and lo and behold, they end up being right.

Your subconscious mind is incapable of distinguishing between an actual event and one that is only imagined. This God-given dynamic of the human brain allows you, through repeated visualizations, to convince your subconscious mind that a desired goal has already been accomplished.

Once your mind believes something to be true, it automatically adjusts your thoughts, words, emotions, and behaviors to be consistent with your visualization. A visualization is a by-product of an electrical and chemical process within the brain. Because your visual images are composed of electromagnetic energy that consists of matter, they are, in effect, real. As a result, your mind and body interpret them as reality and respond to them as though they were actually happening. For example, during mental rehearsals of their events, Olympic athletes often experience physiological changes—increased heart rate, respiration, perspiration, or even involuntary muscle movements—as if they were participating in the real event. Best of all, according to Stanford neurosurgeon and psychologist Dr. Karl Pribram, electromagnetically charged visual images produce a magnetic field that attracts back to the visualizer those things he or she vividly imagines and senses. This phenomenon enables you to attract into your life the very people, resources, and circumstances necessary to translate your goal into concrete reality.

TWO TYPES OF VISUALIZATION

You can visualize two primary aspects of a goal. One is the specific outcome itself; the other is the process or series of steps you must take to get there. It is important to practice both, but if you have to choose, practice outcome visualization. The realization of the actual goal counts the most, not necessarily how you get there.

In *outcome visualization,* you rehearse the achievement of your goal in rich sensory detail. You should focus on the exact moment that represents attaining the goal. Outcome visualization keeps you excited and motivated, especially during the inevitable glitches, delays, or temporary disappointments. The more your eye is on the goal, the more focused and determined you will be.

In *process visualization,* you mentally preview the steps necessary to accomplish your goal. World-class athletes invest the time not only to envision the desired end result but also to see how they want to get there. The more an athlete practices mentally, the better his or her performance becomes. The mind actually trains the body to perform just

Two Types of Visualization

Outcome

Focus on the exact moment that represents attainment of your goal.

Process

Mentally preview the steps or actions necessary to reach your goal.

as it did in the mental rehearsal. Since the mind is the only place where you can practice perfectly, it behooves you to work out there often. The more you see yourself performing effectively, the more comfortable, confident, and relaxed you will feel in the actual event, and the better you will perform. This sense of familiarity breeds excellent results.

The Seven Components of Successful Visualization

Enhancing any of the seven components of effective visualization will expedite the physical manifestation of the visualized image—in other words, will help you realize your goal more quickly.

1. Relaxation. How relaxed you are when you picture something that you want to occur plays a major role in how fast the desired mental image becomes rooted in the subconscious. And it has to be rooted in the subconscious before it becomes a reality. Tension, anxiety, and worry tend to hamper concentration and block the formation of your goals. Before you visualize a goal, take the necessary time to get deeply relaxed. It is very important not to feel rushed or to feel that there is something else more valuable you should be doing.

2. Frequency. The more frequently you visualize a goal, the more that goal will tend to influence the way you think, talk, feel, and act. You will become more likely to engage in activities that move you toward your goal and progressively less inclined to do things that slow your progress. The benefits of every act of visualization accumulate like a giant snowball, generating momentum. The more committed you are to continually previewing your goals on your "personal video screen"—that is, your mind—the more quickly you will experience tangible results.

3. Clarity. The clearer you are about any goal you hope to achieve, the more motivated you will be to accomplish it. Likewise, when you distinctly imagine accomplishing your goal, your enthusiasm, desire, and creativity soar. For example, imagine discussing with your spouse the characteristics of your future dream home. Envision discussing only the size, style, location, number of bedrooms, and price. While that is a good start, imagine the difference in your excitement and motivation to move in when you start considering the special features that appeal to you individually and

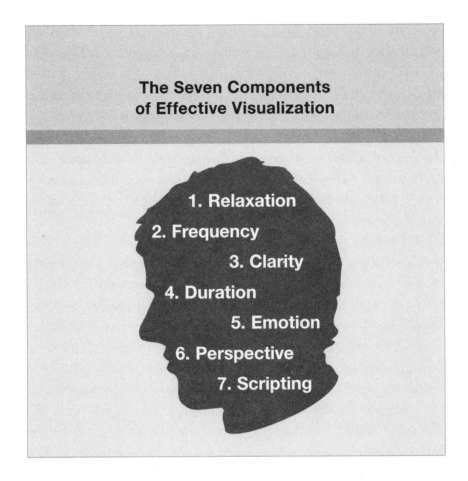

**The Seven Components
of Effective Visualization**

1. Relaxation
2. Frequency
3. Clarity
4. Duration
5. Emotion
6. Perspective
7. Scripting

as a couple. The neighborhood, the master bedroom design, the exercise room, the finished hardwood floors, the automatic hot-water dispenser, the big closet in the garage, and the deck overlooking the garden and pool are all important details that add life to your picture. Considering all the possibilities and envisioning how you will personalize the house into a home help complete the mental equivalent.

Add as much detail to your visualization as possible. Make it graphic, colorful, and vividly rich. The existence of small details makes your mental pictures seem authentic. **The more skilled you become at precisely duplicating in your head what you want to see in your life, the more rapidly you will reach your goals.** The inability to see details in your visualization is a strong clue that you are not making the progress you are capable of.

4. Duration. The longer you can hold on to a crisp, clear picture of your goal, the sooner and more likely it is to appear. Each time you visualize, attempt to hold the picture a little longer than the time before. Refuse to let fear, worry, distractions, or any other type of resistance cut short the length of each act of visualization or your commitment to persevere. All forms of real and imagined resistance begin to dissolve the longer you hold a concrete mental image of the goal you desire. The more you practice visualization, the stronger your ability to concentrate becomes. With practice, you will be able to lock out all extraneous thoughts that dilute the focus of your mental movie.

5. Emotion. The more emotional intensity you can generate while picturing your goals, the faster new mental commands are accepted by your subconscious mind. When you visualize, concentrate on manufacturing the precise feelings that would accompany the accomplishment of your goal. Then amplify, or even exaggerate, those feelings over and over until they are internalized. To produce positive, forceful emotional states, remind yourself of the many wonderful benefits you will receive when your goal is reached. **Mentally celebrate in advance by pretending your goal has already been accomplished.** Drench yourself in the feelings of satisfaction, gratitude, and inner peace you would feel if you actually reached your goal. Take in all the sensations of the experience you are imagining.

6. Perspective. This refers to the point of view you take while visualizing. The perspective from which your mental picture originates influences its overall strength, clarity, and intensity. If, as you visualize, you are looking through your own eyes at the accomplishment of your goal, you are fully associated in your mind. This means you are the player. You are seeing from a participant's perspective. You are in the game and experience all the relevant sensations. This *associated perspective* supercharges your central nervous system with passion, excitement, and exhilaration.

The other perspective is called *disassociation*. When your visualization is disassociated, you are watching yourself through the eyes of a spectator. It is like watching yourself in a home movie. Imagine sitting

The Perspective While Visualizing

The Spectator

Like watching yourself
in a home movie.

Either perspective can be
mastered with patience
and practice.

The Player

You are *in* the game and
experience all the relevant
sensations.

at a traffic light, looking over at the car next to you, and noticing that the driver is you. This is the disassociated, or detached, point of view. While most people have a natural tendency to visualize in one of the two perspectives—associated or disassociated—either perspective can be mastered with patience and practice.

The disassociated perspective is a helpful mental technique for a couple of reasons: First, when practiced, it allows you to see yourself more objectively, similar to watching yourself on video to evaluate your performance. It is often easier to spot flaws and other opportunities for improvement from a distance. That's why great athletes, speakers, and entertainers often review their performances on film. Second, this perspective is useful for minimizing the emotional impact of a prior or upcoming event, when that is desired. Consider that a spectator of a World Series game or the Super Bowl doesn't experience the same intensity of emotions as the players, though he or she can be very involved.

The associated, or fully engaged perspective, should be used when you want to boost the excitement, motivation, and energy of your mental image by being in the game, seeing it through your own eyes.

7. Scripting. It is crucial to have a written script that details every aspect of your visualization. Your script need not be long, but it should contain all the key aspects of the imagined event with as many details as possible. Again, the details bring authenticity to your imagination. **Describing your visualization in writing will force you to crystallize your thinking.** If there are any gaps in your mental picture, they will become apparent as you try to translate your visual story into the written word. I have found with my 1% Club clients that a visualization script often provides the tangible tool that encourages consistent use of an otherwise nebulous exercise. Very few people are disciplined enough to create and implement a visualization exercise regularly without some sort of prompter. The presence of the script tends to make you much more inclined to practice visualization. And the more you practice, the better you get. A good, reasonable script will probably be about one to one and a half typed, double-spaced pages. All essential details should be included, without any extraneous words or phrases.

Here are some ideas to help you pull your visualization script together:

a. *State your specific goal in the form of an affirmation.* Here are some examples:

I effortlessly achieve my ideal body fat percentage of eighteen!

I joyfully earn one hundred thousand dollars or more this year!

I read the Bible from cover to cover by December 31!

We gratefully move into our dream home by March 30!

I safely summit Mount Rainier by July 31!

I easily achieve straight A's this semester!

I take my wife on a surprise weekend trip by June 30!

b. *Consider why reaching this goal is important to you.* What are the benefits? Include specific and nonspecific benefits as well as tangible and intangible benefits.

c. *Imagine the exact moment you accomplish this goal or fulfill your dream.* What event would most represent this accomplishment? Ideas include reaching a mountain summit, taking a romantic getaway, launching a new business, a baptism, a wedding reception, a birth, a family trip, a graduation ceremony, a training certification, a housewarming, an athletic achievement, an awards dinner, an adventure or travel, or a business meeting.

d. *If this were happening right now, how would you feel?* Step into that moment. Pretend you are there right now. What emotions would be most dominant? Perhaps passion, contentment, happiness, excitement, relief, optimism, fulfillment, or confidence.

e. *Who is with you and supporting your accomplishment?* This could be family, coach, business partner, boss, personal assistant, banker, investor, mentor, friends.

f. What do you see around you that is evidence of your accomplishment? Ideas include incredible views, new car, new pool, church altar, teller window, reporters, signed contract, finished drawings, stained-glass windows, TV cameras, photographs.

g. What are you doing? Dancing, depositing, straining, crawling, describing, calling, cheering, toasting, jumping, hugging, smiling, signing, giving, praying.

h. Sounds. What do you hear? Clapping, laughter, triumphant yells, the wind, silence, toasts, congratulations, music, chatter, whispers, ocean waves, "I love you," "I'm proud of you!"

i. Sense of smell. What scents stand out? Chocolate-chip cookies, fresh ink, new car, salty air, her perfume, garlic, sweet-smelling flowers, his cologne, other unique scents.

> In 1990, actor and comedian Jim Carrey wrote himself a check for ten million dollars. He wrote "for acting services rendered" on the check and postdated it Thanksgiving 1995. He carried the check in his wallet, looking at it daily until he signed a ten-million-dollar contract to star in *The Mask 2*—almost a year ahead of his target date.

j. Touch. What are you holding, sitting on, or leaning against? Handshakes, hugs, pats, palm trees, sand, rocks, keyboard, envelope, clothing, pens, fancy glasses, comfortable furniture.

k. Taste. What do you taste? Champagne, cheese, shrimp cocktail, energy bar, pure water, fresh fruit, filet mignon, brownies, chocolate-chip ice cream, peppermint mouthwash, sweat, Gatorade.

l. What words or phrases capture this experience? Success, joy, exhilaration, yes, gratitude, fully alive, satisfaction, contribution.

m. Which of your values are most reflected by what you see? Service, faith in God, wealth, relationships, commitment, family, integrity, adventure, duty, risk, goal setting, stewardship.

All these ideas and questions will help you write a compelling script for your visualization.

When my wife, Kristin, decided she was ready to be a mother (about six months before we officially began trying to conceive), she found a newspaper photograph of a man who closely resembled me (although not quite as handsome!) holding a beautiful baby. Kristin pinned the picture up on a minibulletin board in our shared walk-in closet. Day after day, with barely any effort or intention, we both got a glimpse of the picture. Did it work? Well, of course we both had to do our part, but conception did occur within the first month! I still show this photograph to many of my clients.

Visual Triggers

In addition to mentally rehearsing your goals, it is also effective to surround yourself with visual representations of those goals. Having these visual reminders in your environment is an effortless way to stay focused and motivated. Constantly be on the lookout for Web sites, photographs, quotes, headlines, sketches, and other items that remind you of your goals. The reminders do not have to fit your aspirations exactly; they just need to symbolize your goals. Of course, if you can find exact pictures, those work best. For example, if your goal is to be lean and muscular by reaching your ideal weight, find a picture of yourself when you were lean and put it on the refrigerator door. If you cannot find the right picture of yourself, simply cut out a picture from a fitness magazine of someone who has the look you're shooting for. Keep the picture anywhere you will see it often. In a weight-loss situation, the refrigerator tends to work best. One of my clients took a slightly different approach to improving her health by placing photos of healthy gourmet meals on her refrigerator.

Here are some other examples:

If your goal is to earn $100,000 by December 31, your visualization device might be a picture of a large stack of $100 bills, the numbers *$100,000* written out and colored in, or simply a photograph of something you will buy when you earn the money.

If your goal is to travel to New Zealand, then your visualization trigger will likely be pictures of New Zealand from a travel brochure or magazine, along with the dates you plan to be there.

If your goal is to read the Bible from cover to cover in the next three years, your visualization device might be a digital photograph of yourself sitting in your study with your Bible and a clock in the background that reads 5 a.m. (And maybe a tall mug of hot coffee or tea!)

TRY A GOAL MAP!

A goal map is a large visual reminder of a goal or group of goals you want to accomplish. To create your goal map, attach pictures, photos, sketches, headlines, or other visual stimulators to a poster or bulletin board. Alternatively, if you are so inclined, you could pull together a beautiful version on your home computer. (If you need help, just ask a nearby child!) If you're still doing it the old-fashioned way, print your goal in bold, block letters in the center of the board, using several different colors of ink. Then paste or pin pictures around the statement of your goal. Magazines, brochures, catalogs, and newspapers are good sources to get you started. Some goal maps I've seen are very neat and logically organized, while others are more like a collage. Experiment and see which approach works best for you. I encourage you to intersperse affirmations or quotations with your pictures.

I've used some variation of a goal map for years, and at the very least, it has kept me more motivated, inspired, and enthusiastic. At one point, I had a separate goal map (I use a bulletin board) for each area of my life hung up on the walls of my exercise room. Visualizing and exercising is

> I've encouraged a number of my clients to create and regularly review ideal financial statements that represent where they want to be financially nine, eighteen, and thirty-six years down the road. The money-management software packages available today make this particularly easy. Try putting together your ideal net worth statement for nine or eighteen years from now. Look at it often.

a wonderful combination. (By the way, each of the goals represented on those goal maps has now been accomplished.)

If you don't have much room to devote to your goal map, then try hanging it up on the back of a closet door or sliding it under your bed and pulling it out every night for review before you go to sleep. If you take the digital route with this project, your goal map could be transformed into your screen saver. **By flooding your mind with a constant stream of success images, you displace old self-defeating doubts, fears, and insecurities.**

CREATE A FUTURE SCRAPBOOK

A variation of the goal map is a future scrapbook. It serves the same purpose and can be more private and convenient. Make your future scrapbook a preview of your life's coming attractions. Fill it with pictures, quotations, affirmations, and any mementos that symbolize the course you want your life to take. The scrapbook should be the visual story of your future life. To get started, simply collect pictures and other items, as you would for a goal map, and paste them to sheets of paper or card stock. Then insert them into a three-ring binder. (You might consider laminating the pages first.) A photo album or a photo program on your computer could serve the same purpose. There is virtually no limit on the different approaches to putting together a future scrapbook! Just be creative and review it often, especially right before bedtime and immediately upon arising in the morning.

The more visual cues you can place around you, the more often you will be triggered to think about your goals and the less you will be tempted to think about what you don't want. Also, the very act of searching for the appropriate pictures and reminders of success will stimulate your reticular activating system, which in turn will help you be more alert to the people and resources necessary to transform your dreams into realities. I encourage you to choose a few of these visualization techniques and commit to practicing them over the next thirty days. You'll be amazed at the difference it makes!

Lesson 6 Questions for Reflection

Describe the efforts you have previously made to discipline your mind. Were they successful? Why or why not?

Why is it more common to dwell on your current reality instead of envisioning something far better?

In your experience, do you use your memory or your imagination more frequently? Which might be more effective in encouraging you to reach your goals?

Why are world-class athletes and entertainers the primary practitioners of mental training techniques? What can we learn from them?

Which of your goals are so demanding that you feel compelled to practice visualization and mental rehearsal?

———— ∞ ————

Whom can you influence with the ideas from this lesson in the next forty-eight hours?

LESSON 6 ASSIGNMENTS

1 | Complete a visualization script for one of your top five three-year goals.

2 | Invest ten to fifteen minutes a day in reading the script and imagining that your goal is already a reality.

3 | Collect visual reminders (pictures, quotes, sketches, etc.) for each of your top five goals and place them where you will see them daily.

Choose a Maximum-Energy Lifestyle

Neglect is a silent killer.

In this lesson, you will learn to

- Make health-producing choices

- Develop a positive mental attitude

- Control stress

- Exercise effectively

- Eat for energy

- Sleep for success

- Relax and rejuvenate

Boundless energy is not an accident. Individuals who experience a continuous, revitalizing flow of energy make different choices than those who consistently operate from an energy deficit. You can increase your return on energy and your return on life by becoming highly sensitive to the lifestyle choices you make. Remember, your level of energy equals your level of health. If you are short on energy, you are short on life. Every area of your life will be compromised by a depleted supply of energy. More than any other factor, a lack of energy will cause you to underachieve and underperform. As Vince Lombardi, the legendary Green Bay Packers coach, said, "Fatigue does make cowards of us all." When you are run down, drained, or otherwise out of balance, your choices suffer. You become more oriented around the short term; you think more about what is expedient than what is in your long-term best interests. You act defensively and reactively.

God designed your body intricately. When you manage it wisely—by eating right, avoiding harmful substances, getting enough sleep, and exercising regularly—you will have better health and more energy. But, as the book of Isaiah explains, the ultimate source of energy is God. "Those who trust in the LORD will find new strength. They will soar high on wings like eagles. They will run and not grow weary. They will walk and not faint" (Isaiah 40:31, NLT).

Abundant levels of energy are the indispensable prerequisite for individual achievement, success, and peace of mind. Fortunately, becoming a high-energy, high-output human being need not be a gamble. The causes of vigorous energy have been thoroughly researched and well documented. Superior levels of vitality come naturally from implementing the causes of maximum energy outlined in the rest of this lesson.

Seven Keys to a High-Energy Lifestyle

1. WRITE DOWN A GOAL FOR HOW LONG YOU WANT TO LIVE HEALTHFULLY AND PRODUCTIVELY.

Obviously, your life is in God's hands. However, you do have control over many choices that can significantly affect your life expectancy and overall health. With that in mind, I encourage you to set a goal to live at least to the age of ninety. Then begin to organize your lifestyle around health habits that are consistent with that goal. The best way to do this is to take a sheet of paper and draw a line down the center. On the left side, write down everything you can do that will help you live to at least age ninety.

On the right-hand side, write down all the negative habits or activities you may be tempted to engage in that would hurt your chance of living a long life. Once you complete the list, begin to eliminate all the negative health habits one by one, and begin introducing or reinforcing the positive health habits.

> Everything can be taken away from a man but one thing: the last of the human freedoms—to choose one's attitude in any given set of circumstances, to choose one's own way. —*Viktor Frankl*

2. DEVELOP AN ULTRA-POSITIVE ATTITUDE!

Your attitude is the habitual way you think. Over the long haul, the quality of your life will be determined by the quality of your attitude. A maximum-energy lifestyle requires that you choose a positive mental attitude. This is not something that happens to you; it is a deliberate choice that ultimately becomes a habit. The more positive you are, the more energy you will have. **You become positive by deciding in advance that you will always choose the most resourceful response to any given set of circumstances.** This means that even if you are justified to do otherwise, you will always take the high road, choosing to act in a manner consistent with the goals you want to reach and the person you want to become.

Difficult, trying times reveal just how positive you really are. Think about it. What's the virtue in being positive when you're on a roll, when everything is clicking for you and going your way? Your potential for business excellence, excellence in your marriage, and excellence in your family life demands that you master the skill of staying U.P. (ultrapositive) even when—and especially when—everyone else isn't.

When you're ultra-positive, you'll be more creative, productive, en-

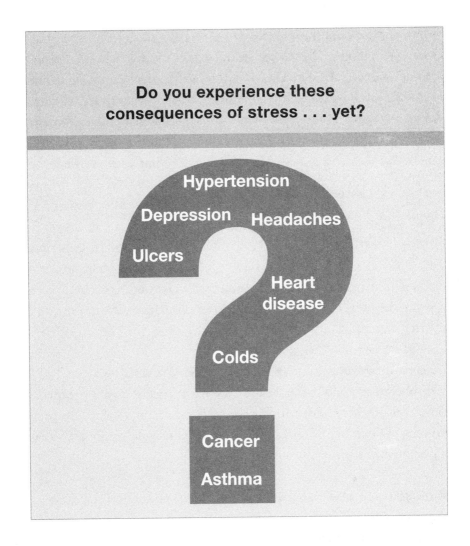

ergetic, attractive, and most importantly, receptive to God's will. Here are seventeen practical strategies to get you started.

a. Make the decision to stay U.P.

Nothing of consequence happens until you promise yourself that you'll become the most positive person you know. Raise your standards! Everything else flows from this key decision to separate yourself from the 99 percent who blame, whine, gossip, and predict doom and gloom. Life is short. Take a stand.

b. Start U.P. and end U.P. every day.

One of the simplest ways to transform your attitude is to begin and end each day with what we in The 1% Club call Positive Mental Nutrition Feed your mind with inspirational, spiritual, and/or motivational ideas for ten to fifteen minutes immediately upon awakening each morning and right before drifting to sleep each evening. As mentioned in lesson 5, during these two time periods, your mind is extremely susceptible to programming, so make sure your inputs are positive, healthy, and goal directed. Read, visualize, affirm, pray, and rewrite your goals!

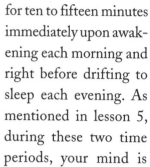

> Some things are within our control, and some things are not. It is only after you have faced up to this fundamental rule and learned to distinguish between what you can and can't control that inner tranquility and outer effectiveness become possible. —*Epictetus*

c. Summarize each day's victories, large or small, in writing.

This one practice alone can transform your attitude and generate quantum leaps in self-confidence. Start logging your accomplishments each evening in a notebook or hardbound journal or on your computer. What a positive habit!

d. Increase your physical exercise.

Another pillar of ultra-positive living is consistent, moderate exercise. This includes aerobics to burn fat and improve heart health, weight training to tone and strengthen your muscles and elevate metabolism, and flexibility exercises to stay loose and limber. Face the facts: When you're in terrific shape and feel better about yourself, you feel better about your life. You're positioned to live up to your full potential. We'll discuss this in more detail later in this lesson.

e. Break up the big four.

Negative thinking leads to negative emotions, which in turn trigger more negative thinking. The vicious cycle becomes engaged. The top four negative emotions include fear, worry, blame, and guilt. These terrorize your potential and immobilize your efforts toward becoming ultra-positive. When you begin experiencing results you didn't want or expect, it's easy to get scared and start thinking more about potential losses than potential gains. This mind-set triggers worry, or what I call reverse goal setting, where you vividly imagine what you *don't* want. To transfer the burden of worry, you will often blame someone or something outside of yourself. Alternatively, you may exaggerate your role in the negative events and experience guilt. Consider negative emotions to be lies from the enemy. Deal with them directly by refusing to entertain the thoughts that fuel them. This is a point very much worth reinforcing: **Invest your time in thinking about what you want instead of what you don't want.**

> [Jesus said,] "That is why I tell you not to worry about everyday life—whether you have enough food and drink, or enough clothes to wear. Isn't life more than food, and your body more than clothing? Look at the birds. They don't plant or harvest or store food in barns, for your heavenly Father feeds them. And aren't you far more valuable to him than they are? Can all your worries add a single moment to your life?" *(Matthew 6:25-27, NLT)*

f. Forgive someone, including yourself, daily.

Harboring grudges and hostility against anyone, including yourself, tends to attract more circumstances to be upset about. Practice forgiving somebody every day for real or imagined transgressions. The better you become at forgiveness, the more positive you can become as a human being. If you skip this one, I'll forgive you.

g. Quarantine negativity if you can't dissolve it.

Carve out a particular time and place to worry (worry time) and to complain (issue time) each week. This is extremely effective because then the rest of your week isn't diluted with the minority of negative circumstances that can infect otherwise healthy days. When you cut the spontaneity out of negativity, you severely weaken it.

h. Focus on God. He's U.P.

Remind yourself of everything you know to be true about God. God is all-powerful. God is love. God is sovereign. God is always with us. God is absolute truth. God never changes. And so on. Thinking about God is good!

i. Schedule four-minute positive injections every two hours.

Think of these as positive pit stops. Review your goals or mission. Practice affirmation or visualization. Pray. Read the Bible. Relive a positive memory. Write a thank-you card or send an e-mail of appreciation to someone important.

j. Simplify and declutter to stay U.P.

Complexity is negative. Simplicity is positive. Room by room, drawer by drawer, try tossing out one tiny item of clutter every day for thirty consecutive days. My 1% Club clients love this one, and so will you, because doing even a small task will help you feel more positive. Break your jumbo-sized goals into subgoals and milestones, and then splinter them into even smaller pieces if necessary to spur you into action. Renegotiate or downsize existing commitments to lighten your load a bit for the next thirty days.

k. Get to bed sixty minutes early for ten straight days.

Fatigue, especially chronic fatigue, invites negativity and cowardly thinking. During periods of intense or prolonged stress, extra sleep will help your brain remain an ally in the war against mediocrity. Cut something out of the evening schedule, and drift to sleep with visions of victories dancing in your head. Your body, mind, and spirit will thank you.

l. Take a twenty-four-hour mental fast.

Become ultra-positive one day at a time. You can rid your attitude of toxic thoughts through the practice of mental fasting. (Make sure to read my book *The 4:8 Principle* if you want to master this unconventional and very powerful mental technique.) During your fast, abstain

Benefits of Consistent Aerobic Exercise

1 | Improves sleep

2 | Relieves stress

3 | Burns fat

4 | Suppresses appetite

5 | Enhances attitude

6 | Stabilizes chemical balance

7 | Fortifies immune system

8 | Heightens self-esteem

from all complaining, criticizing, excuse-making, gossiping, and worrying whatsoever! Start with a sixty-minute fast, and gradually build up to disciplining your mind to repel all negativity for a full day. Focus on progress. Repeat as necessary.

m. Stay U.P. and watch your favorite funny movies.

Laughter is fabulously positive. Research indicates that people who laugh more actually have more fun. Is that surprising? Consider building your own comedy library on DVD. Watch often. You'll stay healthier, more creative, and less stressed—and that's a great alternative to the medicine cabinet.

n. Have a counterattack plan ready.

Become hypersensitive to your thought life. Since you can be negative only when you're thinking negative thoughts, you can quickly become positive by thinking positive thoughts. I referred to this earlier when I explained the principle of substitution. The split second you notice any negative thought running through your mind, replace it emphatically with something like "I am responsible" or "I trust God" or "I can do it." Repeat, repeat, repeat! Be ready with a positive comeback before the heat of the moment. Make negative, limiting thoughts unwelcome in your mind.

o. Re-engage an old hobby to stay U.P.

Involve yourself in a positive activity that used to be important to you but may have been squeezed out of your life due to other priorities. This will be both therapeutic and rejuvenating. Consider it a gift to yourself.

p. Intentionally cultivate ultra-positive company.

This one is mandatory. It's next to impossible to become or stay U.P. when the people you live or work with are petty, negative thinkers. Nothing equals the influence of your habitual associations. Be purposeful about which people are close to you. As you become more positive, you will attract more positive people in your life, and that's good.

q. Help someone else stay U.P.

Donate your money. Donate your time. Volunteer. Simply serve someone less fortunate or contribute your talents and gifts to a worthy organization. Helping those who need help reduces self-centeredness and puts your own challenges into a much more positive perspective.

The key to staying U.P. is to remember that every situation can be positive when you view it as an opportunity for growth and self-mastery.

Now let's look at the next way to develop a high-energy lifestyle.

3. CONTROL STRESS.

We experience negative stress when we feel out of control of the sequence of events in our lives. It's like being in a fast-moving car without a steering wheel. We experience stress when we live inconsistently with what we have identified as most important to us. **Most of all, we**

experience stress when we recognize that we are living far beneath our potential.

The inability to deal effectively with stress has been linked to cancer, asthma, headaches, depression, cardiovascular disease, the common cold, ulcers, hypertension, chronic fatigue, and immune-system suppression, to name but a few conditions. Mounting research indicates nearly 80 percent of all illness can be linked at least partially to psychological stress.

Stress is a subjective condition. What causes some to get stressed-out causes others to get excited and creative. Some people thrive on change, while others avoid change and the stress that goes with it at all costs. Big things cause stress for some while the accumulation of little things is stressful for others.

Ask yourself this question: "Have I ever been stressed-out when I wasn't thinking stressful thoughts?"

I can guarantee you have not. It would be impossible. The bottom line on stress is this: The way you interpret your circumstances triggers a stress response. The meaning you place on a certain event makes it stressful, not the event itself. Start paying closer attention to the way you habitually describe mistakes and unpleasant situations to yourself and others. Finding a positive angle on a negative situation goes a long way toward minimizing stress. The very act of searching for something good redirects your attention and keeps you in a productive, resourceful state.

Remember, the way you think about something makes it stressful. Stress doesn't really exist except to the degree to which you allow it. Your thoughts create emotions, which in turn mold your thinking. Your thoughts, via neurochemicals, electrical charges, and trillions of special receptors, influence every cell in your body. This is how conditions on the outside, negatively interpreted, produce harmful physiological changes on the inside.

Unless you deliberately develop an effective, perpetual system for stress management, you will undercut your performance and face greater risk of disease.

Here are some tips to get you started:

- Follow all the other keys to a maximum-energy lifestyle outlined in this lesson.

- Practice mental discipline. Choose what you think about. (Review lesson 5.)

- Make a personal stress inventory. Write down all the current stressors in your life and one step you could take to alleviate each one. Accepting that a difficult situation is real and clearly identifying the root problem is an important step. Proper diagnosis is half the cure.

- Simplify your life. Eliminate and concentrate. Focus on the vital few things that contribute the most to your overall life satisfaction. Taking on too much or spreading yourself too thin inevitably leads to a sense of overload.

4. COMBINE AEROBIC, STRENGTH, AND FLEXIBILITY EXERCISES.

If you want maximum levels of energy, take responsibility for becoming a mini-expert on exercise and fitness. Subscribe to the most credible health and exercise magazines, add informative fitness sites to your Web favorites, and build your own library with the latest books, DVDs, and other resources related to energy and wellness.

Aerobic exercise

The most important component of effective exercise is aerobic exercise. Aerobics, or cardiovascular endurance, refers to the sustained ability of the heart, lungs, and blood to perform optimally. Through consistent aerobic conditioning, your body improves the way it takes in, transports, and uses oxygen. This means your heart and lungs will be stronger and more efficient at performing their functions. Proper aerobic exercise causes your body to burn fat, while anaerobic exercise causes the body to burn glycogen and store fat. Many people unknowingly exercise anaerobically when they intend to exercise aerobically. This results in, among other things, a frustrating retention of fat. The intensity of your exercise is what makes it anaerobic or aerobic.

Consistent and proper aerobic exercise has the following benefits:

- improves quality of sleep
- relieves stress and anxiety
- burns excess fat
- suppresses appetite
- enhances attitude and mood
- stabilizes chemical balance
- heightens self-esteem

Each of the above benefits either directly or indirectly leads to high levels of both mental and physical energy.

Here are some tips for maximizing the quality of your aerobic workouts:

Work out aerobically four to six times a week for at least forty-five minutes.

Use the talk test to stay within your target heart rate and gain the maximum fat-burning benefits. Your exercise intensity should allow you to work out steadily while still being able to talk without gasping for breath. For even better results, invest in a heart-rate monitor to track your cardiovascular progress more precisely.

Use a calm, steady, enjoyable pace. Correct aerobic intensity is strenuous but still pleasurable.

Instead of stretching your cold muscles before exercising, spend three to five minutes warming up by doing light, easy motions that mimic your sport or aerobic activity. Then do some stretching.

Also, take about five minutes to cool down gradually after your workout. Never stop exercising suddenly. Following your workout, keep moving at a progressively slower and slower pace. This cooldown period allows your heart rate and body systems to return safely to their pre-exercise state.

Vary your aerobic routine throughout the week, or at least from week to week. Alternating between several different aerobic activities develops a more balanced state of fitness and prevents boredom, which ultimately leads to the sofa and the remote control.

Drink lots of water before, during, and after aerobic exercise. Purified water is best, and research indicates that ice-cold water activates the metabolism better, even though room-temperature water enters the digestive track faster. Plan ahead so that ample water is convenient and accessible.

Whenever possible, blend your aerobic workout with a mental workout by listening to inspirational music or self-development CDs, or visualizing your goal achievement. Try to think healthy, energetic, and empowering thoughts because this will energize you and complement your physical workout. As tempting as they may be, avoid news channels and newspapers as you exercise. I encourage you to make your workouts completely positive experiences.

Strength Training

The next component of effective exercise is strength training. Proper strength training improves muscle tone, balance, coordination, and of course overall vibrancy. Including strength training, or progressive resistance training, in your workout regimen will help you burn extra fat, resist fatigue, and avoid nagging injuries. You will also look and feel better.

Muscle is the primary energy burner in your body, so the more toned you are, the more excess body fat you will burn in a twenty-four-hour period. With less fat, you will be more energetic. And with more strength, you will develop more endurance for work and everyday tasks, leaving you with additional energy for other enjoyable relationships, projects, and activities.

Flexibility

Flexibility is the loneliest component of intelligent exercise because it is left out most often. Proper stretching energizes the body and the mind. As my Choi Kwang Do instructor repeatedly told me, a flexible

Steps to High-Energy Nutrition

1 | Plan your meals.

2 | Eat low-fat or nonfat foods.

3 | Eat balanced meals and snacks.

4 | Eat seven or more servings of fiber-rich fresh fruits and vegetables daily.

5 | Limit the white poisons: sugar, salt, bleached flour.

6 | Drink lots of water.

7 | Supplement your diet with an all-natural, high-quality vitamin and mineral formula.

body equals a flexible mind. Done properly, stretching reduces tension, promotes circulation, improves posture and balance, increases range of motion, and helps prevent injuries. In addition, it is invigorating. In light of all the obvious benefits, it just might be worth adding yoga, Pilates, or some type of martial arts to your overall fitness plan. These disciplines involve significant flexibility and core stability.

After stretching, you'll be more active and productive. Here are some guidelines for effective stretching:

Remember that before stretching you should do very light movement that mimics your sport or exercise activity. This increases blood flow to your muscles and makes them supple, limber, and prepared for stretching.

Stay relaxed throughout all stretching exercises. This requires a deliberate effort at first. Repeatedly tell yourself that you are relaxed, flexible, and resilient.

Slowly move in and out of each stretch. Avoid bouncing. A few stretches held for a minute or two each is far more useful than ten stretches held for ten seconds each.

Breathe slowly, deeply, and continuously. Holding your breath promotes tenseness.

Go at your own pace. Enjoy and don't rush.

5. EAT FOR MAXIMUM ENERGY.

The foods you choose to eat throughout the day exert a powerful impact on your level of physical, mental, and emotional energy. Fortunately, your nutrition is within your control! What you allow to pass between your lips will impact your health and well-being, either positively or negatively. It is your responsibility, as we teach in The 1% Club, to stay on top of the latest scientific research concerning the foods you eat and their connection to your energy, immunity, and longevity. You cannot rely on this book alone, government recommendations, one new study, or any other single source of information.

Upgrading your nutritional philosophy and daily habits based on the practical, test-driven suggestions in this lesson will cause you to experience a quantum leap in your hour-to-hour energy levels. This will quickly translate into more quality time with those you love and for the projects and goals that you find most meaningful.

It is worth mentioning here that after age thirty, it is virtually impossible to compensate for mediocre nutrition with aggressive exercise. In other words, the older you get, the easier it is to out-eat your exercise program. The really good news, though, is that just a few small changes in your diet can cause you to wake up your metabolism and experience a surge of mental and physical vitality.

Here are some steps to high-energy nutrition:

a. **Take the time to plan your meals.** Planned meals are much more likely to include smart nutritional choices that promote energy, health, and well-being. Most Americans find themselves in such a constant rush that what they eat is based on convenience rather than nutrition. **Planning meals puts you back in control.** It is also likely to save you time and money at the grocery store and help you avoid impulse buys. Learn to read and understand food labels so that you know what you're really paying for.

b. Focus on balanced nutrition. The food you eat—specifically the quality and the balance of proteins, fats, and carbohydrates known as macronutrients—dictates your body's biochemistry. Your biochemistry then regulates metabolism, energy, immunity against disease, performance, and ultimately longevity. The primary factor in achieving optimal health and fat-burning is *stable blood sugar*. And balanced nutrition is the key to stabilizing your blood sugar. Balanced nutrition requires simply that you incorporate each of the macronutrients into each meal or snack.

For example, a balanced dinner could include salmon or chicken as the lean protein, a spinach salad mixed with a variety of fresh vegetables as the carbohydrate, with an olive-oil-based dressing as the essential fat. Add a tall glass of sparkling water with a slice of lemon, and you're set! It is really that simple, and you will feel the difference immediately. A balanced lunch could include a turkey burger as the lean protein, a small bowl of homemade vegetable soup along with half of a whole-wheat bun as the carbohydrate, and an optional slice of avocado as the essential fat. A balanced breakfast could include an Egg Beaters omelet with Canadian bacon and 2 percent cheddar cheese as the protein, a slice of whole-wheat toast as the carbohydrate, and a small handful of raw almonds as the essential fat. A balanced snack could be an apple with a few raw cashews or your favorite raw nuts. Another snack could be several celery sticks dipped in raw almond butter or nonhydrogenated peanut butter.

Of course, the options are virtually endless, and you will be much more successful with a definite plan.

In The 1% Club, we teach our members to make a peak-performance shake with these ingredients:

- lean, complete whey protein isolate

- low-glycemic fresh or frozen fruit

- an omega- or flax-oil blend

This shake tastes fantastic and is a powerful way to start your day or energize yourself in the middle of the afternoon. For our latest 1% Club recommendations and a free copy of our shake recipes, please visit www. successisnotanaccident.com.

At optimal levels, blood sugar is your body's primary source of energy. It is the gas that fuels your cells. Your cells and tissues need glucose, just as your lungs need air. Without it, you couldn't survive. For your body to function at its peak, it must keep blood sugar levels in balance—neither too high nor too low. This is critical. Either too much or too little sugar profoundly affects your health, energy levels, and mood. Once you discover the perfect balance of lean complete proteins, essential fats, and low-glycemic carbohydrates for your body, you can achieve maximum energy, fat loss, and vibrant health—for the rest of your life!

c. Eat frequent small meals and very light snacks. Large meals overburden your digestive system and interfere with absorption of nutrients. Big meals, especially those high in saturated fat, trans fat, or refined foods, lead to postmeal lethargy and low performance. If you are serious about generating more energy, make your breakfast the biggest and most nutritionally sound meal of the day. When you enjoy breakfast within thirty or forty-five minutes of rising, your body and brain will function better and your energy level will stay more consistent into the evening. Eating a healthy breakfast also jump-starts your metabolism and decreases the likelihood of binge eating later in the day. Balancing high-fiber carbohydrates with lean complete proteins and healthy fats for breakfast sets the right nutritional tone for a world-class day. Lunch should be slightly smaller but still a balance of the right macronutrients. Dinner should be the lightest of your three main meals, while still following the balance of carbs, proteins, and fats. Most Americans do the reverse—a small breakfast and a large dinner—which makes little sense from a physiological or performance standpoint. Experiment with a light midmorning and midafternoon snack. This will boost mental performance and physical endurance and will curb overeating at dinnertime. If you eat an early supper, a balanced late-night snack will help

Seven Keys to High Energy

1 | Set a goal for how long you want to live.

4 | Exercise effectively.

2 | Maintain a positive attitude.

5 | Eat for energy.

3 | Control stress.

6 | Sleep for success.

7 | Take time for rejuvenation.

keep your blood sugar stable and tend to improve the quality of your sleep.

d. Work in at least seven servings of fresh fruits and vegetables throughout your small meals, shakes, and snacks during the day. Fruits and vegetables are naturally high in vitamins, minerals, fiber, antioxidants, and the recently discovered phytochemicals that protect the body from cell damage. Go for the most colorful combinations of fruits and vegetables, as this indicates richer nutrient content. A lunch or dinner salad packed with lots of your favorite vegetables is an easy way to accomplish this. Also, make sure you have plenty of washed fresh fruit and veggies on hand in your kitchen.

e. Drastically reduce or eliminate sugar, salt, and refined white flour. Collectively—and deservedly—these are referred to as the three white poisons because they offer little if any nutritional value and are known to contribute to a host of health problems. The body has no need for added sugar, yet the average American consumes nearly two hundred pounds of simple sugar every year in the form of desserts, breakfast pastries, soft drinks, candy, jams, syrups, and alcohol, just to name a few. In addition to hampering the fat-burning process, simple sugars—often disguised as corn syrup, maltose, dextrose, dextrin, honey, or molasses—reduce your appetite for high-nutrition foods and leave you feeling even more tired and sluggish after the initial pick-me-up wears off. This is primarily the result of blood-sugar imbalances.

The human body also needs little or no additional salt, yet many products on supermarket shelves have salt as a primary ingredient because of its preservative value. Many people also pour excessive amounts of salt on their food even before tasting it. By relying only on the natural salts found in your food, you'll start to enjoy a wider range of flavors that were previously neutralized with excessive salt. In addition, you'll maintain a healthy balance of sodium to potassium, which helps prevent cancer, heart disease, high blood pressure, and strokes.

Bleached or refined white flour, the third white poison, has been stripped of virtually all vitamin content and just about all fiber. It is, in

Seven Tips for Better Sleep

1 | Arise at the same time every day.

4 | Develop a calming bedtime routine.

2 | Eat for deep sleep.

5 | Put your to-do list together early.

3 | Reserve the bedroom for sleep and sexual relations with your spouse.

6 | Hide the clock!

7 | Identify your most comfortable sleeping temperature.

effect, nutritionally dead. All white-flour products, white rice, pasta, and crackers should be replaced with their whole-grain equivalent and enjoyed only in moderation. Though many white-flour products claim to be enriched with vitamins, just remind yourself what made them white.

f. Drink lots of water. Two-thirds of the composition of the human body is water, and water is involved in every function of the body. It helps transport nutrients and waste products in and out of cells. It's required for all digestive, absorptive, circulatory, and excretory functions, as well as for the utilization of the water-soluble vitamins. Water also helps us maintain proper body temperature. Additionally, water suppresses the appetite and helps the body eliminate stored fat. We often mistake thirst for hunger, and an unnecessary intake of calories is the result. When you feel hungry but don't think you should be, try rapidly drinking several cold glasses of water. If you wait ten minutes or so, often the food craving will pass. Quickly drinking several large glasses of ice-cold water is also a terrific energy booster. Try it and see.

To determine how much pure water you need each day, simply divide your body weight in pounds by two. The quotient is the minimum number of ounces of water you need to consume each day. For example, if you weigh 150 pounds, your body needs at least seventy-five ounces of water over the course of the day. If you exercise vigorously or drink alcohol or caffeine, you may need even more water to ensure that your body has what it needs to maintain peak health and vibrant energy.

g. Supplement your diet with an all-natural, high-quality multiple vitamin and mineral formula. Even if you eat a well-balanced diet, manage stress well, and exercise regularly, it is still a good idea to protect yourself with the nutritional insurance provided by a broad-spectrum vitamin, mineral, and antioxidant supplement. Be sure to check the expiration date on the bottle to ensure maximum freshness. I'm a strong believer in natural food supplements and have been using a synergistic combination for many years. I encourage you to learn all you can about vitamins and supplements, and begin working them into your overall high-energy fitness strategy.

6. SLEEP FOR SUCCESS.

Sufficient, refreshing sleep is essential to a high-energy lifestyle. Your body needs sleep to repair itself and function properly. As you sleep, you dream, allowing your subconscious to sort through unresolved psychological and emotional issues. Brain waves slow down, blood pressure falls, muscles relax, the immune system is boosted, damaged tissues and cells are repaired, and the pituitary gland produces more hormones. Without sufficient sleep, the body is more likely to break down.

How much sleep you need depends on your unique makeup as well as the other lifestyle choices you make. Research indicates that individuals who effectively deal with stress and negative emotions need less sleep than those who are stressed-out or worry chronically. Some people function best with only five to six hours of sleep while others may need as much as ten hours. On average, the most effective rest tends to come from seven to eight hours of sleep. Improving the quality of your sleep can usually reduce the quantity of sleep you need.

Sleeping poorly night after night, or partial sleep deprivation, is a major cause of chronic low energy. Here are some tips for achieving optimum sleep:

a. Arise at the same time every day. Don't sleep in on the weekends, at least not more than an hour. It confuses your body's biological clock. Oversleeping reduces alertness and energy in much the same way as jet lag. You reduce the amount of time you're awake, making it tougher to fall asleep the next night.

b. Eat for deep sleep. Avoid caffeine products four to five hours prior to sleep. If you drink alcohol, finish not less than three to four hours before bedtime. While alcohol immediately makes some people drowsy, it actually interferes with normal brain-wave patterns of sleep, preventing deep, revitalizing rest. Also, always eat a light evening meal. This will prevent your body from using too much energy for digestion while you're trying to get deep sleep. As mentioned earlier in this lesson, if you eat an early dinner, consider a very small but balanced nighttime snack. This encourages a smoother transition into deep sleep while preventing a drop in blood sugar during the night that could disturb your rest.

c. Reserve the bedroom for sleep and sexual relations with your spouse. Your bedroom should be a comfortable, ultra-relaxing haven designed for peacefully letting go of the day. Avoid intense discussions, brainstorming, snacking, TV watching, financial planning and budgeting, and all work when you're in your bedroom. These types of activities promote excitement or agitation and work against a good night's sleep. When you allow only two activities in your bedroom, you condition yourself for successful sleep.

d. Develop a calming bedtime routine. You must have a workable system in place that helps you unwind and let go of the day. Applying relaxation techniques; listening to classical music or nature sounds; or praying, reciting affirmations, or reading inspirational material contributes to optimal sleep. Research also indicates that a hot bath or shower or moderate exercise within three hours of bedtime can significantly deepen sleep.

e. Put together your to-do list early, preferably before entering your bedroom and several hours before going to bed or while still at work. Nothing encourages insomnia more than waiting until the morning to write down all that needs to be done. If ideas do come to you after the lights are out, then go ahead and unload them onto your list or into a digital recorder. It only weakens your sleep to try to remember all that needs to be done the next day.

f. Hide the clock! Put your alarm clock where it can be heard but not seen. Difficulty sleeping is only exacerbated by having a clock to look at, highlighting how late it is. No one sleeps well under time pressure. Also, avoid getting jolted awake with a blaring alarm. How you awaken and what you do in those first few minutes sets the energy and performance tone for the rest of the day. Experiment with a positive music or affirmation alarm with the volume set just loud enough to notice it. Decide at night what you want your first thought of the next day to be. Make it an inspiring thought, and repeat it to yourself as you drift off to sleep. I wake up each morning with the first thought of "This

Seven Tips for Replenishing Mental Energy

1 | Take frequent five-minute stress breaks.

4 | Take two weeks of vacation annually.

2 | Take one day every week away from all work.

5 | Declutter your home, car, and office.

3 | Take a four-day vacation every quarter.

6 | Get a massage.

7 | Recultivate simple pleasures.

is the day the Lord has made. [I] will rejoice and be glad in it" (Psalm 118:24, NLT). Another energizing first thought could be, "I believe that something wonderful is happening to me today!" You'll be amazed as this thought races to your consciousness when you awake. Remember, you're in charge of your attitude. Don't leave it to chance.

g. **Identify your most comfortable sleeping temperature.** Sixty-five to seventy degrees tends to work best for most people. Invest in a firm, supportive mattress and arrange for a very dark, quiet bedroom. Dim light and slight noise can damage the quality of your sleep, even if you never wake up completely. Sleeping on your side in a semifetal position with a supportive neck pillow tends to reduce tossing and turning.

7. REST AND REJUVENATION.

In addition to getting proper sleep, you need to schedule ample time to revitalize your mind. Optimum creativity and productivity require mental rest. This means that your brain, like your body, needs sufficient recovery and renewal to operate at its peak. Unless you balance periods of intense mental work with periods of doing nothing, or margin, you are likely to experience chronic mental fatigue. This begins with a feeling that you're not accomplishing enough and usually coincides with periods of high stress or mental and physical exhaustion. To compensate for the lack of accomplishment, you put in more time and push yourself even harder. This makes you even more tired and ineffective, which leads to putting in even more hours, and so on. The quantity and especially the quality of your creative projects drop as your focus and judgment fade. You might believe that you are actually crunching out good work, but it's just an illusion. In addition, mounting fatigue and a tense, overtired state tend to spill over into your family life, generating more impatience and irritability. No skill is as valuable to your overall creativity, vitality, and well-being as learning to disengage from the compulsion toward constant busyness. Here are tips for letting go and replenishing your mental energy:

a. **Take frequent, five-minute stress breaks** during the day to redirect your thinking to something fun and undemanding. Unplugging

Top Ten Energy Leaks

10 | *Alcohol.* Alcohol is an extreme carbohydrate and contains a lot of calories. It's also a depressant, a diuretic, increases appetite, slows metabolism, and can damage the organs.

9 | *Caffeine.* Don't panic; you can still have your coffee as long as you limit yourself to a cup or two per day. Caffeine is a diuretic. It also stimulates the pancreas to produce insulin, a hormone that regulates blood sugar. When too much insulin is released at once, the body's blood-sugar level plunges rapidly, resulting in cravings.

8 | *Irregular sleep,* whether too much or too little. Aim for between seven and nine and a half hours of quality sleep each night. Go to bed and wake up at consistent times each day.

7 | *Ineffective exercise.* Whether you exercise inconsistently or not at all, you're not giving your body the workout it needs. Another pitfall for some people is overexercising and undereating. Find the right balance.

6 | *Eating just three times per day.* Forget the old paradigm of three large meals. Eating smaller amounts five or six times a day prevents binging, stabilizes blood sugar, and cranks up your metabolism.

5 | *Skipping breakfast.* Breakfast is the most strategic meal of the day, and skipping it is devastating to your energy for the rest of the day. From an energy standpoint, you cannot recover if you blow off breakfast.

4 | *Boredom.* This is the opposite of passion and can occur when you feel in a rut in your career, your marriage, or your faith. If you're feeling bored, look for a creative new approach.

3 | *Overeating.* Large meals overburden your digestive system, stealing energy from goal-directed activity. Even overeating healthy foods causes excess insulin production, encouraging fat storage and leaving you feeling sluggish.

2 | *Dehydration.* Your body is more than two-thirds water, and your brain is 85 percent water. Even if you're just one percent dehydrated, your energy level drops off.

1 | *Negativity.* Harboring unhealthy emotions like fear, anger, worry, and guilt—or any sort of "stinking thinking"—will drain your energy. If you're going to plug any of these leaks, plug this one first. Before you can strengthen your body, you must strengthen your mind. Every thought and feeling has an energy consequence.

And, of course, smoking, which is outrageously obvious and offensive to your energy goals.

from the day's current activity for just several minutes at a time will be surprisingly invigorating. Here are some ideas:

Visualize a vacation.

Review Bible verses.

Think about your childhood.

Flip through a catalog or photo album.

b. Take at least one twenty-four-hour period a week when you do no intense mental or work-related activity. Research indicates this is more effective than working straight through.

c. Take a four-day vacation every ninety days. Completely shut off your mental gears and refrain from doing any work. Remind yourself that rejuvenation is not just a reward for high performance; it is a prerequisite as well. Lose the guilt!

d. Take at least two weeks of vacation each year during which you do no work or mentally demanding activity. Even if you really, really love what you do, it is simply not possible to relax and work. Dabbling in light work on a vacation defeats the rejuvenating process. Whenever possible, take the two weeks consecutively. If you have been driving yourself aggressively, it may take almost a week just to unwind. The second week is most therapeutic.

e. Declutter your home, car, and office. Having stuff scattered throughout your physical surroundings adds to stress levels and makes you overwhelmed. Straightening up your environment can improve your sense of control and enthusiasm for life. Developing a systematic process of simplifying and streamlining your possessions can be refreshing and energizing.

f. Consider massage to release pent-up tensions and benefit the mind, body, and emotions. In addition to seeing a professional massage therapist, learn self-massage techniques so that massage can become a weekly habit. An hour is wonderful, but ten to fifteen minutes gets the job done.

g. Recultivate the simple pleasures of life: conversation, family dinners and walks, reading together, music, stars, sunset, poetry, gardening, photos, home movies, journaling, and solitude.

Think about it. Without your health, the pursuit of your goals can come to a screeching halt. And without enough energy, even a modest goal can seem like an insurmountable challenge. Now, though, you have plenty of ideas and strategies for boosting your overall health and vitality. It is my hope that you will now select the suggestions from this chapter that resonate with you and start putting them into practice immediately. When you do, you will experience an amazing increase in the levels of energy that fuel your mind, body, and spirit, as you continue to follow God's purpose and plan for your life.

Lesson 7 Questions for Reflection

Who are the three highest-energy people you know, and what habits do they practice consistently?

In what ways could you be more of a blessing to your family if you had an extra fifty-five minutes of productive energy each day?

What excuses do most people have for not exercising? Why are these excuses not valid?

What did Vince Lombardi mean when he said, "Fatigue does make cowards of us all"? What could this mean to you and your future?

What would have to happen for you to become the most well-educated person you know in the area of health and nutrition?

──────── ∞ ────────

Whom can you influence with the ideas from this lesson in the next forty-eight hours?

LESSON 7 ASSIGNMENTS

1 | Set a goal for how long you desire to live healthfully and productively (determine your age and the year).

2 | Make a list of all the lifestyle choices that are consistent with living productively and healthfully until your target age.

3 | Make a list of all the choices that are not consistent with living to your life-span goal.

4 | Write on a note card the following self-talk statement: "My daily choices create my perfect health." Tape this note card to your bathroom mirror.

Tomorrow Changes Today!

Congratulations!

Now that you've reached the end of *Success Is Not an Accident,* you are at the beginning of a new chapter in your own life. Armed with the time-tested principles and concepts you've just learned, you are ready to take your entire life to a much higher level and truly honor the potential you were blessed with at birth. While this quest is, no doubt, a lifelong pursuit, it must start today with just one person—*with you*—as you take action on the ideas you have just read. By changing your choices, you will change your life. Your future, however, does not improve tomorrow. I have observed that the unhappiest people in the world seem to talk the most about what they intend to do tomorrow. This mind-set is not for you! Your future gets better *now*. **Tomorrow changes today!**

In the Introduction, I mentioned that *Success Is Not an Accident* was written to be internalized. Have you accomplished this yet? Once these ideas are internalized, *you* own them. They become *your* ideas. They become second nature. They become part of who *you* are. When this occurs, you find yourself naturally putting these principles into practice. You choose to succeed and become a greater blessing to others. You choose who you intend to become and then you write down goals that will steer your life in that predetermined and purposeful direction. You choose to invest your time wisely so that you achieve what God wants you to achieve. You choose to get out of your own way and build beliefs that make success inevitable. You choose positive visualization because you know that positive results follow positive mental pictures. Finally, you choose a maximum energy lifestyle to ensure that you have the fuel of achievement. When do you make these choices? You make these choices today. **Tomorrow changes today!**

Over the years, I've received hundreds of letters and e-mails from readers all over the globe who have read *Success Is Not an Accident* multiple times. This seems to be an approach worth imitating. These readers report to me that they take away a new insight each time they reread the book. More important, though, they report extraordinary improvements and results across each area of life. These types of breakthroughs for readers of *Success Is Not an Accident* are widespread, and they are certainly possible for you as well. I truly hope you've learned what you intended to learn when you first opened this book. As your coach, let me challenge you to take just a moment to evaluate your understanding and application of the seven lessons outlined in *Success Is Not an Accident* with a quick review below. Rate yourself on a scale of 1–10 (with 10 being the highest):

_____ **Lesson 1: Choose Success.** Do you fully understand the connection between your choices and the life you are living today? Do you believe that God wants you to succeed? In what ways has your success already blessed others? Have you written your personal definitions of success and mediocrity?

_____ **Lesson 2: Choose Who You Want to Become.** Have you given much thought to how the world could be different because of your particular life? Do you believe God had one specific thing in mind when he made you? Do you have a personal mission statement written in the present tense as if it were true today?

_____ **Lesson 3: Choose to Write Down Compelling Goals.** Have you brainstormed 150 life goals in writing? What are your top five goals right now? Can you clearly and concisely explain to the important people in your life why goal-setting is essential to maximizing your full potential? Why do so many resist setting goals?

_____ **Lesson 4: Choose to Invest Your Time Wisely.** Do you sense that you are spending or investing most of your time? How frequently do you verbalize the phrase, "I didn't have time"? Have you calculated the cost of misusing just fifteen minutes a day over one year? Are you keeping a record or time log to specifically track how you use your time?

_____ **Lesson 5: Choose to Get Out of Your Own Way.** Do you talk more about what you want or what you do not want? Are you aware of "the first rule of holes"? Is your self-talk in alignment most of the time with the person you are striving to become? What would you believe about yourself, which you don't believe today, if you had already achieved your most important goals?

_____ **Lesson 6: Choose Positive Visualization.** Have you developed a visualization script for at least one of your most important goals? Can you explain why positive results tend to follow positive mental pictures? Have you started to surround yourself with visual reminders of your goals? How do images of victory and success help tame doubts, fears, and insecurities?

_____ **Lesson 7: Choose a Maximum-Energy Lifestyle.** How long would you like to live healthfully and productively? What current lifestyle choices do not support that longevity goal? Have you already developed an effective system for managing stress in your life? Have you ever been stressed out _without_ thinking stressful thoughts? What are your sources for trustworthy information about health and nutrition?

How did you do? Did you isolate some strengths or weaknesses? Did you identify some areas for further study? I imagine you've learned a lot, maybe even more than you originally anticipated. However, the reality is that simply learning something new has very little if any practical value. It is only when you begin to make better choices that your life gets better. Things don't improve by themselves. It is only when you begin to think and then act differently that worthwhile improvement and positive change occurs. You were born. That was not your choice. And you have no choice about dying, either. What you do in the interim, though, is completely up to you.

The presence of a thoughtful, written plan for each of your goals is the clearest evidence that you are a serious participant in your own life, that you are determined to make a difference in between those two choices over which you have no control. With a carefully crafted plan, you distinguish yourself from the masses that hope and wish and even pray for more joy, passion, and success, but never do anything to help create it. Think back to lesson 3, *Choose to Write Down Compelling Goals.* Did you identify the goals that are important to you?

Do you want to strengthen your relationship with God?
Show me your plan!

Do you want to get leaner and healthier in the next year?
Show me your plan!

Do you want to connect at a much deeper level with your spouse?
Show me your plan!

Do you want to live a life full of adventure and passion?
Show me your plan!

Do you want to eliminate clutter and complexity in your life?
Show me your plan!

Do you want to exert much greater influence with your children?
Show me your plan!

Do you want to work less and still earn more?
Show me your plan!

An extraordinary life is simply the accumulation of thousands of efforts, often unseen by others, that lead to the accomplishment of worthwhile goals. Regardless of your personal financial situation, remember that you are most definitely rich with choice. And your choices reveal who you really are. More than any other single factor, you are where you are today because of the choices you have made. To achieve things you have never achieved before, you must take action today that you've never taken before. **Tomorrow changes today.** Consider these examples from my coaching practice at The 1% Club. I've witnessed numerous clients

- Work less and earn even more income
- Decide to have a third or fourth child
- Repair and renew damaged family relationships
- Discover their passion and change careers
- Commit their life to Christ
- Recommit to a previously troubled marriage
- Leave the ministry and enter the business world
- Leave the business world and enter the ministry
- Find and marry the person of their dreams
- Lose 20, 30, even 40 pounds and keep the weight off
- Enjoy the vacation of a lifetime
- Run marathons and Ironman Triathlons
- Summit some of the highest peaks around the world

None of these achievements is an accident. Each of these personal break-throughs is the result of one thing. Making a different choice based on the principles explained throughout this book. These choices are not made in the future. They are made right now, in the present moment. And, only you have the power to make the choices that will accumulate into the fruits of an exciting, successful, and satisfying life.

. . . What will you do?

Tomorrow changes today.

Get started now.

Thought Triggers

General

1 | What do you want to do, have, or become?

2 | If you knew you couldn't fail, what great cause would you pursue wholeheartedly?

3 | What is your God-sized dream?

4 | What is the most significant change you'd like to create in your life?

5 | Whom would you like to meet and have lunch with?

6 | How could you significantly increase your service and contribution to others?

7 | What's on your "Before I Die" list?

Spiritual

1 | What are your spiritual disciplines now? What should they be?

2 | Would you like to read the Bible from cover to cover?

3 | Would you like to teach a Sunday school class?

4 | Are you living the life God gave you?

5 | Who's holding you accountable in your spiritual walk?

6 | What's standing between you and a closer relationship with God?

7 | What will have to happen for you to experience peace of mind?

Physical

1 | How could you become a better steward of your body?

2 | What foods produce the most energy for your other goals?

3 | How could you take better care of your brain?

4 | How many hours of physical, mental, and emotional energy do you want to have each day?

5 | How fit do you want to be at age 75?

6 | What are your favorite types of physical exercise?

7 | Would you like to have your workout room in your house?

Marital

1 | What is the goal of your marriage?

2 | What books or audio programs could increase your wisdom about relationships?

3 | How could you reduce or eliminate stress in your spouse's life?

4 | What are the strengths of your marriage? Weaknesses?

5 | What romantic experience could you enjoy together in the next year?

6 | What is the most unconventional thing you could do to take your marriage to the next level?

7 | What are your most productive habits as a couple?

Parental

1 | What is the goal of your parenting?

2 | Who, besides you and your spouse, influences your children on a regular basis? Is this okay?

3 | What habits would you like to see ingrained in your children when they become adults?

4 | How could you build a stronger relationship with each of your kids?

5 | What qualities are essential for a successful family?

6 | What is your family culture like today? What should it be like?

7 | What do your children learn about God from you?

Financial

1 | Do you know what you need to know about managing your money?

2 | What would you like your net worth to be when you're 50? 60? 70? 80?

3 | How much money do you need to enjoy your ideal lifestyle?

4 | How much money would you like to give away in your lifetime?

5 | What causes would you like to support financially?

6 | What fears, worries, or insecurities do you have about wealth?

7 | What are you teaching your kids about money?

Career

1 | What impact do you want to make on your profession, and how will you measure this?

2 | What do you need to learn in order to rise higher in your field?

3 | Who is mentoring you in your business career?

4 | What other types of professional opportunities would you like to explore?

5 | Would you like to start your own business?

6 | How could you create an income source from one of your hobbies?

7 | Are you more interested in security or opportunity?

Personal Development

1 | How much of your annual income do you budget for personal and professional development?

2 | What are the next twelve books you are planning to read?

3 | What courses or retreats are you currently registered for?

4 | How could you use time in the car to learn and stay inspired?

5 | What types of lessons would you like to take? (cooking, computer, flying, scuba diving, guitar, martial arts, dancing, hang gliding, etc.)

6 | What is the most recent positive habit that you have developed?

7 | Do you meet with a Mastermind group each week or month?

Just for Fun

1 | How could you have more fun with the important people in your life?

2 | What amenities would you like to be surrounded with at home?

3 | What updates would you like to see in your wardrobe?

4 | What new technology might simplify your life at home?

5 | What is your dream car?

6 | What home chore or task would you like to delegate?

7 | How would you spend a $50,000 bonus within twenty-four hours if you had to spend it on yourself?

Travel

1 | What are five sights you would like to see during your lifetime?

2 | What is your dream vacation with your spouse?

3 | What is the ideal vacation for your family?

4 | What cultures would you like to experience?

5 | How could you transform your next vacation into an unforgettable memory?

6 | What well-known hotels would you like to stay in?

7 | What modes of travel would you like to experience?

Relationships

1 | How strong is your relationship with God today?

2 | How intentional are you in choosing your friendships?

3 | With whom do you spend most of your free time?

4 | What are your strengths as a friend? How could develop them further?

5 | Which of your friends is the most positive influence on you?

6 | Describe your ideal mate. How do you need to change to attract your ideal mate?

7 | In light of your long-term goals, with whom should you invest more time?

Adventures*

1 | What would you do with an extra three weeks of vacation each year?

2 | How could you get out of your comfort zone and come alive?

3 | What mountains would you like to climb?

4 | Would you like to ride in a submarine or hot air balloon?

5 | What great sites would you like to photograph?

6 | What adventures could you share with your spouse? with your kids?

7 | What fears could you face and overcome in the next year?

---

*For a glimpse of the exciting lifetime goals of legendary achiever John Goddard, visit **www.1percentclub.com/goddard.**

NOTES

Lesson 1: Choose Success
1. Ralph Waldo Emerson, "Prudence," in *Essays* (1841).
2. Orel Hershiser with Jerry B. Jenkins, *Out of the Blue* (Brentwood, Tenn.: Wolgemuth & Hyatt, 1989), 65.
3. Orel Hershiser with Robert Wolgemuth, *Between the Lines: Nine Principles to Live By* (New York: Warner Books, 2001), 6.
4. Ibid., 57.
5. Ibid., 123.
6. David L. Chancey, "Why Do We Keep Daddy Around," *The Citizen*, http://www.thecitizen.com/archive/main/archive-000618/fp-06.html, June 18, 2000.
7. Hershiser, *Out of the Blue,* 3.

Lesson 2: Choose Who You Want to Become
1. James Allen, *As a Man Thinketh* (New York: Putnam, 1987), 13.

Lesson 3: Choose to Write Down Compelling Goals
1. "Georgia Biographies: David Perno, Baseball Head Coach," http://www.georgiadogs.com/ViewArticle.dbml?SPSID=46824&SPID=3589&DB_OEM_ID=8800&ATCLID=324031&Q_SEASON=2006, December 21, 2006.
2. David Perno, interview with author, January 30, 2003.
3. Ibid.
4. "Ron Polk—Head Baseball Coach," http://www.mstateathletics.com/index.php?s=&url_channel_id=15&url_subchannel_id=&url_article_id=5279&change_well_id=2, December 21, 2006.
5. Ibid.
6. Perno, interview with author.
7. Ibid.
8. Denis Waitley, *Seeds of Greatness: The Ten Best-Kept Secrets of Total Success* (New York: Pocket, 1983), 144.

Lesson 4: Choose to Invest Your time Wisely
1. William Shakespeare, *Hamlet,* Act 3, Scene 4.

Lesson 5: Choose to Get Out of Your Own Way

1. "About Scott Adams: Biography of Scott Adams 2," Dilbert.com, http://www.dilbert.com/comics/dilbert/news_and_history/html/biography2.html, January 16, 2003.
2. Scott Adams, *The Dilbert Future: Thriving on Stupidity in the Twenty-first Century* (New York: HarperBusiness, 1997), 246.
3. Andrew Shalit, "A Kind Word," *Chicken Soup for the Soul at Work: 101 Stories of Courage, Compassion, and Creativity in the Workplace* (Deerfield Beach, Fla.: Health Communications, 1996), 58.
4. Adams, *Dilbert Future*, 249.
5. Henrietta Anne Klauser, "There's a Very Simple Way to Achieve Your Goals . . . Just Write Them Out," *Bottom Line,* June 1, 2000, 13.

ABOUT THE AUTHOR

Tommy Newberry is the founder and head coach of The 1% Club, an organization dedicated to helping entrepreneurs and their families maximize their full potential. As a pioneer in the life-coaching field since 1991, Tommy has equipped business leaders in more than thirty industries to work less, earn more, and enjoy greater satisfaction with the right accomplishments.

Tommy is the author of *The 4:8 Principle, 366 Days of Wisdom & Inspiration,* and numerous audio programs, including the best-selling series Success Is Not an Accident: Secrets of the Top 1%. Known for his blunt, highly practical, and no-nonsense coaching style, Tommy has earned the title of America's Success Coach. His passion for developing the whole person is clearly evident throughout his live workshops, keynote presentations, books, and audio courses. Tommy's annual Couples Planning Retreat takes world-class planning tools into the family realm, allowing husbands and wives to design a more balanced, simplified, and enriching life together.

An avid goal setter, Tommy has earned certification as an emergency medical technician and PADI rescue diver, as well as a black belt in the Korean martial art of choi kwang do. He lives in Atlanta with his wife, Kristin, and their three boys. If you want to contact Tommy, please visit www.tommynewberry.com.

The 1% Club's SuperFOCUS Program

Join other like-minded individuals in The 1% Club's SuperFOCUS Program. In just a half day every quarter, you'll evaluate your progress, share breakthrough ideas, and build unstoppable momentum toward your biggest goals. This one-of-a-kind coaching program keeps your entire life on purpose, energized, and organized around the few things that matter most.

BEYOND JUST LEARNING!

This is not a seminar, a lecture, or a one-time event. Though you are certain to learn a lot during and between the quarterly workshops, this program is not about what you learn; it is about what you do differently. The SuperFOCUS is a one-of-a-kind group coaching experience that helps you strategically assess your present circumstances so that you will operate more effectively and consistently in the future.

WE STICK WITH YOU . . . YOU FOLLOW THROUGH!

Unlike one-day or weekend events, The 1% Club emphasizes follow-through and sustained positive change. As pioneers in the life-coaching field, we know that peak performance is not created from a motivational rally or from an inspirational class alone, but from ongoing exposure to

- the right people
- the right ideas
- the right tools, and
- the right encouragement.

The cumulative effect of repeated reinforcement, constructive feedback, and authentic accountability produces long-lasting results. You will also benefit from our experience in more than thirty diverse industries. We combine, filter, and share with you the best insights and strategies from other members of The 1% Club, so you gain a decisive advantage. From these true-life success stories, you will learn what really works in the field. For more information, please visit www.1percentclub.com/superfocus.

Who's Coaching You?

Your success strategy doesn't end with a single book. Continue on your path toward personal excellence and lifelong fulfillment with The 1% Club's *Virtual Coach* program.

No travel. No workshops to attend. No schedule conflicts!

The *Virtual Coach* program keeps you playing your "A" game in each area of life. Regardless of where you live or work, you can tap into the ongoing power of The 1% Club with a minimum investment and on your own time schedule. Anytime, anywhere, you can learn, plan, practice, and implement these life-changing concepts—at your own pace and when it's convenient for you. Best of all, we'll stick with you over the long haul, pushing and challenging you to break through previous plateaus. If you can't be with us in person, this is the next best thing.

No more going it alone with this timeless system! We'll stick with you from start to finish. From weekly reminders and monthly performance advice to quarterly conference calls, we'll support you, step-by-step, toward your best year ever—and far beyond. Our mission is simple: to help you maximize your God-given potential in all areas of life. We've helped thousands already . . . *why not let us help you help yourself?* Anchored in the core principles of *Success Is Not an Accident*, the *Virtual Coach* equips you to

1. Clarify your most significant goals
2. Organize your life in alignment with your top values
3. Consistently nurture your most important relationships
4. Define your goals in such a way that you will naturally accelerate your progress
5. Stay on track, focused, and free of distractions
6. Overcome procrastination and other potential-limiting behaviors
7. Maximize physical, mental, and emotional energy
8. Reduce stress, tension, and worry
9. Refine your unique strengths
10. Build unstoppable self-confidence for the right risks
11. Eliminate clutter and other junk that bogs you down
12. Upgrade your earning, investing, and giving.

With this advanced coaching system, Tommy Newberry helps you build instant momentum and equips you to take command of yourself and your future—starting immediately. As a special thanks to readers of this book, enroll for a limited time with promo code "VCSUCCESS" and save $100 on registration. Learn more at www.1percentclub.com/virtualcoach, or call 1.888.663.7372, toll-free.